GLOBAL WARMING

A case study in groupthink

How science can shed new light on the most important 'non-debate' of our time

Christopher Booker

ISBN 978-0-9931190-0-2

Contents

Foreword

By Professor Richard Lindzen

The bizarre issue of climate catastrophism has been around sufficiently long that it has become possible to trace its history in detail, and, indeed, several excellent recent books do this, placing the issue in the context of a variety of environmental, economic and political trends. Darwall's *Green Tyranny: Exposing the Totalitarian Roots of the Climate Industrial Complex* and Lewin's *Searching for the Catastrophe Signal: The Origins of The Intergovernmental Panel on Climate Change* deserve special mention in this connection. Booker's relatively brief monograph asks a rather different but profoundly important question. Namely, how do otherwise intelligent people come to believe such arrant nonsense despite its implausibility, internal contradictions, contradictory data, evident corruption and ludicrous policy implications. Booker convincingly shows the power of 'groupthink' to overpower the rational faculties that we would hope could play some role. The phenomenon of groupthink helps explain why ordinary working people are less vulnerable to this defect. After all, the group that the believers want to belong to is that of the educated elite. This may have played a major role in the election of Donald Trump, which depended greatly on the frustration of the non-elites (or 'deplorables', as Hillary Clinton referred to them) with what they perceived to be the idiocy of their 'betters'.

Booker's emphasis on the situation in the UK is helpful insofar as there is nowhere that the irrationality of the response to this issue has been more evident, but the problem exists throughout the developed world. The situation everywhere has been reinforced by the existence of numerous individuals and groups that have profited mightily from the hysteria (including academia, where funding predicated on supporting alarm has increased by a factor of about 15–20 in the US), but why so many others have gone along, despite the obvious disadvantages of doing so, deserves the attention that Booker provides.

Professor Lindzen was Alfred P. Sloan Professor of Meteorology at the Masschusetts Institute of Technology until his retirement in 2013. He is a member of GWPF's Academic Advisory Council.

About the author

Christopher Booker has been writing on climate change and energy issues in the *Sunday Telegraph* and elsewhere over the past 11 years. In 2010 his history of the science and politics of global warming, *The Real Global Warming Disaster: is the obsession with climate change turning into one of the most costly scientific blunders in history?* was ranked by *The Bookseller* as one of the UK's three top best-selling books on the environment in the previous decade, alongside titles by Al Gore and James Lovelock.

Born in 1937, he read history at Cambridge and was the founding editor of *Private Eye* between 1961 and 1963. His other books have included *The Neophiliacs: a study of the revolution in English life in the Fifties and Sixties* (1969), *The Seven Basic Plots: why we tell stories, a psychological analysis of storytelling* (2004), *The Great Deception*, a history of the European Union (co-written with Dr Richard North), and *Scared to Death: Why scares are costing us the earth* (2007). In 1979 he made an acclaimed BBC television documentary, *City of Towers*, tracing the crucial influence of Le Corbusier on the post-war redevelopment of Britain's cities.

Author's personal note

Having now written extensively about the global warming issue for over a decade, I kick myself that I did not discover the book that inspired this paper until 2014. When I finally came across Irving Janis's seminal analysis of 'groupthink', I realised just how much more it helped to explain about the story I and many others had been following for so long.

In particular, if I had known about it when in 2009 I published my history of the great alarm over manmade climate change, *The Real Global Warming Disaster*, it might have been a very different book.

Here, more briefly, I look at that story again, brought up to date, but this time showing how Janis's theory adds a whole new dimension to our understanding of one of the most remarkable and puzzling episodes in the history of both science and politics.

It is only by obtaining some sort of insight into the psychology of crowds that it can be understood how powerless they are to hold any opinions other than those which are imposed upon them.

Gustave Le Bon, *The Crowd*

As long as one is within a certain phenomenology, one is not astonished and no one wonders what it is all about. Such philosophical doubt only comes to one who is outside the game.

C.G. Jung, *Psychology and National Problems*

Executive summary

By any measure, the belief that the earth faces an unprecedented threat from 'human-induced climate change' has been one of the most extraordinary episodes in the history of either science or politics. It has led scientists and politicians to contemplate nothing less than a complete revolution in the way mankind sources the energy required to keep modern industrial civilisation functioning, by phasing out the fossil-fuels on which that civilisation has been built.

But for 30 years the way this has all come about has given expert observers cause for increasing puzzlement. In particular they have questioned:

- the speed with which the belief that human carbon dioxide emissions were causing the world dangerously to warm came to be proclaimed as being shared by a 'consensus' of the world's climate scientists;
- the nature and reliability of much of the evidence being cited to support that belief;
- the failure of global temperatures to rise in accordance with the predictions of the computer models on which the 'consensus' ultimately rested.

But there was also the peculiarly hostile and dismissive nature of the response by supporters of the 'consensus' to those who questioned all this, a group that included many eminent scientists and other experts.

The purpose of this paper is to use the scientific insights of a professor of psychology at Yale back in the 1970s to show the entire story of the alarm over global warming in a remarkable new light. The late Professor Irving Janis analysed what happens when people get caught up in what he termed 'groupthink', a pattern of collective psychological behaviour with three distinctive features, that we can characterise as rules.

- A group of people come to share a particular view or belief without a proper appraisal of the evidence.
- This leads them to insist that their belief is shared by a 'consensus' of all right-minded opinion.
- Because their belief is ultimately only subjective, resting on shaky foundations, they then defend it only by displaying an irrational, dismissive hostility towards anyone daring to question it.

This paper begins by showing how strongly all these three symptoms were in evidence, right from the start, when, in the late 1980s, the belief that a rise in carbon dioxide levels was causing the earth dangerously to warm was first brought to the world's attention.

It shows how the rules of groupthink continued to be in evidence when, during the period around the first report of the UN Intergovernmental Panel on Climate Change (IPCC) in 1990 and the Rio 'Earth Summit' of 1992, global warming became adopted as an international scientific and political 'consensus'.

The presence of groupthink was confirmed at Kyoto in 1997, when practical steps were first agreed to slow down the rise in world temperatures, by means that would require the richer, developed nations of the West to reduce their carbon dioxide emissions, while allowing the still 'developing' nations, such as China and India, to continue increasing them until their economies had caught up with the West. Eventually, as the paper will show, this division between the West and the rest of the world would turn out to be the crux of the whole story,

For some years the 'consensus' theory continued to seem plausible, as carbon dioxide levels and global temperatures continued to rise together, just as the computer models on which the 'consensus' relied had predicted. In 1998 temperatures were the highest on record, coinciding with an unusually strong El Niño event in the Pacific.

But then came the 'hockey stick' controversy, which first drew charges that, to make their case seem more plausible, supporters of the 'consensus' – strongly endorsed by the IPCC – were having to manipulate crucial scientific evidence. Their response to these allegations was further evidence of Janis's third rule, that any attempt to challenge the 'consensus' must be ignored, rejected and suppressed.

Between 2004 and 2007, the 'consensus' still seemed to carry all before it, as its claims for the threat posed to the planet by global warming became ever more exaggerated and extreme, as exemplified in Al Gore's documentary *An Inconvenient Truth* and the IPCC's Fourth Assessment Report in 2007.

But it was at this time that more serious cracks began to appear in the 'consensus' case. There had been the continuing failure, since the El Niño year of 1998, of global temperatures to rise as the computer models had predicted: this was what became known as 'the hiatus' or 'the pause'. There were telling examples of how irrationally supporters of the 'consensus' had reacted when they were, for the first time, confronted by world-ranking scientists who were outside the groupthink.

Even more important, there was the emergence through the internet of a new 'counter-consensus', led by technical experts qualified to challenge every scientific claim on which the 'consensus' relied. It was this which, in accordance with Janis's third rule, prompted supporters of the 'consensus' to vilify anyone daring to disagree with them as just 'climate deniers' who were 'anti-science'.

In 2009/2010, the 'consensus' suffered its three most damaging blows yet:

- the release of the Climategate emails between the little group of scientists at the heart of the IPCC establishment;
- the collapse in Copenhagen of the long-planned bid to agree a new global climate treaty, again essentially because of a division between developing nations and the West;
- a series of scandals that revealed that the most widely-quoted and alarming claims in the 2007 IPCC report had not been based on science at all, but on claims made in press releases and false reports put out by climate activists.

On both the Climategate emails and the IPCC scandals the 'climate establishment' did all it could to hold the line, with a series of supposedly 'independent' inquiries staged by its supporters. But the damage had been done. Between 2010 and 2014, despite efforts by supporters of the 'consensus', such as the BBC and the UK Met Office, to keep the alarm going, it became clear that it was no longer possible to sustain the hysteria that had reached its climax in the years before Copenhagen.

But then, as this paper shows, came what amounted to a last throw by the 'consensus', with the approach of yet another major global climate conference in Paris in 2015. The prelude to this, coinciding with another record El Niño event in 2015/2016, was such a rise in global temperatures as to prompt claims that 'the pause' had ended. But expert analysts across the world found that wholesale 'adjustments' had been made to the figures in the main surface temperature records, giving an impression that the global temperature trend had been rising much more than was justified by the original recorded data.

Then came an event as significant as any since the alarm over global warming had first arisen. Documents supplied by every country before the Paris conference, known as INDCs, or 'Intended Nationally Determined Contributions', set out their intended future energy policies. Buried in technical details, these made clear that, however much the countries of the West might be planning to reduce their 'carbon' emissions, the rest of the world, led by China and India, was planning by 2030 to build enough fossil-fuel power stations to increase global emissions by almost 50 percent. China was intending to double its emissions, India to triple theirs.

In other words, the rest of the world had no intention of going along with the declared aim of Paris, to agree on the wholesale 'decarbonisation' of the world's economy. Yet astonishingly, so lost were developed countries in the groupthink that the Western media failed to recognise what was happening.

One person who did was President Trump who, to the fury of all those still blinded by the groupthink, gave the refusal of the rest of the world to reduce its carbon dioxide emissions as his reason for pulling the US out of the Paris Accord (although even now this was not picked up by those reporting on his decision in the West).

Before coming to its conclusions, this paper will briefly summarise some of the immense political consequences of the alarm over global warming: the costs and futility of the steps being taken, chiefly in the West, to switch from fossil fuels to 'low-carbon' sources of energy.

The conclusions then follow, under three headings. The first summarises the nature of the groupthink that has for 30 years come to dominate virtually all public discussion of global warming in the West. The second considers the factors that will make it so difficult for the West to escape from this intellectual straitjacket.

But the final section highlights how the events of the past two years, culminating in Trump's rejection of Paris, have in fact been the crux of the whole story. The rest of the world, led by the fast-growing economies of China and India, has made clear that, whatever the West may continue to believe or do, it is carrying on regardless. This was what Trump recognised when, in July 2017, he finally called the bluff of one of the most damaging examples of groupthink the world has ever known. From now on, the story can never be the same again.

1 Introduction

Since we have now been living with the debate on global warming for 30 years, it might seem hard to imagine that any wholly new scientific perspective could usefully be brought to bear on it. But such is the purpose of this paper, which seeks to use the insights of a distinguished former professor of psychology at Yale to show the real nature of that debate in a startling new light, helping us to understand much that observers have long found baffling.

By any measure, the consequences of the belief that human activity may be causing our planet dangerously to warm have marked it as one of the most extraordinary episodes in history. Countless billions of dollars gone into attempts to confirm the theory that human emissions of carbon dioxide and other greenhouse gases are posing an unprecedented threat to the future of life on Earth. This idea has been found so persuasive by many of the world's politicians that they have been prepared to commit us to spending trillions more on every kind of measure designed to avert that threat.

Their central aim has been, as they put it, to 'decarbonise' the world's economy. They want us to phase out the fossil-fuels on which mankind's material progress has been based for 200 years, and to rely instead on 'carbon-free' sources of energy, such as 'renewables' and nuclear power. Together, they believe, this will bring about such a reduction in human emissions of carbon dioxide that it will have a significant influence on the earth's climate.

This, of course, is why the warming thesis has become so hugely important to all our futures: it has led to the widely accepted view that our planet can only be saved by a fundamental revolution in the way the human race manages its affairs, based on eliminating precisely those sources of energy on which our modern industrial civilisation has been built.

But there has long been a very serious puzzle at the heart of how the discussion of all this has unfolded. From the moment these views exploded to the top of the global agenda in the late 1980s, they might have seemed to carry all before them. But right from the start, a number of reputable scientists found them far from convincing or well-founded. Yet so powerful was the momentum behind what had almost immediately been proclaimed as a 'consensus' of scientific opinion that any questioning of it was swept aside.

Over the years other experts emerged to challenge not just the 'consensus' itself, but the methods being used to promote it: not least the graphs and predictions produced by those computer models which were so central to the case for anthropogenic warming. Equally questioned were the methods being adopted by politicians to counter the supposed threat, such as pouring colossal subsidies into new sources of 'zero-carbon' energy.

But however authoritatively many of these attempts to question the 'consensus' were put, they were automatically dismissed as scarcely worth answering. In other words, the most obvious characteristic of the supposed 'debate' over climate change was that it was never really a debate at all.

There was never any proper engagement between the two sides, because the supporters of the 'consensus', who included all the world's major scientific institutions and most of the media, simply could not accept that any further discussion was called for. Scarcely had the story begun than we were repeatedly told that 'the science is settled'.

For many observers, however, there was something very odd about this: not just the absence of dialogue between the two sides, but the peculiar hostility shown by supporters of the 'consensus' towards anyone who did not share their view. This was not what might have been expected over what was, on any count, one of the most significant issues of the age. So what might explain it? Was there perhaps some clue in human psychology which might help better to explain the extraordinarily one-sided nature of this 'non-debate'?

At this point, step forward Irving Janis, a professor of psychology at Yale University in the 1970s, the man who has given us the crucial missing perspective that may allow us to see this familiar story in a wholly new light.

2 Janis's theory of groupthink

> I use the term 'groupthink' as a quick and easy way to refer to a mode of thinking that people engage in when they are deeply involved in a cohesive in-group, when the members' strivings for unanimity override their motivation to realistically appraise alternative courses of action. Groupthink is a term of the same order as the words in the newspeak vocabulary George Orwell presents in his dismaying *1984* – a vocabulary with terms such as 'doublethink' and 'crimethink'. By putting groupthink with those Orwellian words, I realise that groupthink takes on an Orwellian connotation. The invidiousness is intentional, Groupthink refers to a deterioration of mental efficiency, reality testing and moral judgment.
>
> Irving Janis, *Victims of Groupthink*, 1972

Janis's unique contribution to science lay in his disciplined analysis of what happens when human beings get caught up in an instance of what he called 'groupthink'. Of course, this is a word now casually used all over the place, to dismiss the shared mindset of any group of people with whose opinions one doesn't agree. And Janis himself did not originate the term, which is attributed to William Whyte Jr. in 1952. But Janis minted it afresh by consciously adapting it from George Orwell's 'doublethink' in *Nineteen Eighty-Four*. And what made his contribution so valuable was that, in his book *Victims of Groupthink* in 1972 (in a later edition shortened to just *Groupthink*),[1] he showed that there is a scientific structure to the rules by which groupthink consistently operates.

In fact the only reason why his book is not much better known is that he does not himself seem to have been aware of how much more generally relevant his insights were than to just the subject of his original study. The subtitle of his book was *A Psychological Study of Foreign Policy Decisions and Fiascos*, and the examples he used to illustrate his thesis were all notorious failures of US foreign policy between the 1940s and the 1960s. These included the failure of America to heed intelligence warnings of the Japanese attack on Pearl Harbour in 1941, General McArthur's fateful decision to advance into North Korea in 1950, President Kennedy's backing for the CIA's disastrous Bay of Pigs invasion of Cuba in 1961, and President Johnson's decision in 1965 to escalate the war in Vietnam. In a later edition he added President Nixon's involvement in the Watergate affair.

But what Janis more generally showed through each of his carefully researched case studies was how this form of collective human psychology operates according to certain clearly identifiable rules. Janis several times set out lists of the 'symptoms of groupthink', and his lengthy study included much analysis of its other attributes. But for our present purpose, we can draw out from his work three characteristics of groupthink that are absolutely basic and relevant to our theme. I carefully use here the phrase 'draw out from' because Janis himself nowhere explicitly states that these are the three basic rules of groupthink. But they are implicit in his analysis throughout the book, and form the core of his theory as to how groupthink operates.

3 The three rules of groupthink

Rule one is that a group of people come to share a common view or belief that in some way is not properly based on reality. They may believe they have all sorts of evidence that confirms that their opinion is right, but their belief cannot ultimately be tested in a way that confirms this beyond doubt. In essence, therefore, it is no more than a shared belief.

Rule two is that, precisely because their shared view cannot be subjected to external proof, they then feel the need to reinforce its authority by elevating it into a 'consensus', a word Janis himself emphasised. To those who subscribe to the 'consensus', the common belief seems intellectually and morally so self-evident that all right-thinking people must agree with it. The one thing they cannot afford to allow is that anyone, either within their group or outside it, should question or challenge it. Once established, the essence of the belief system must be defended at all costs.

Rule three, in some ways the most revealing of all, is a consequence of that insistence that everyone must support the 'consensus'. The views of anyone who fails to share it become wholly unacceptable. There cannot be any possibility of dialogue with them. They must be excluded from any further discussion. At best they may just be marginalised and ignored, at worst they must be openly attacked and discredited. Dissent cannot be tolerated.

Janis showed how consistently and fatally these rules operated in each of his examples. Those caught up in the groupthink rigorously excluded anyone putting forward evidence that raised doubts about their 'consensus' view. So convinced were they of the rightness of their cause that anyone failing to agree with it was aggressively shut out from the discussion. And in each case, because they refused to consider any evidence that suggested that their two-dimensional 'consensus' was not based on a proper appraisal of reality, it eventually led to disaster.

The collective refusal to heed intelligence warnings allowed the Japanese to attack Pearl Harbour with impunity. McArthur's hubristic decision to advance into North Korea predictably brought China into the war, with deadly results. The reckless acceptance by Kennedy and his little circle of intimate advisers of a crackpot CIA plan to invade Cuba led inevitably to an embarrassing fiasco. The massive stepping up of US forces in Vietnam produced a response that was to suck the US into ten years of frustration and a growing nightmare, which only ended with their humiliating withdrawal in 1975.

But Janis then followed this litany of failure with two examples of US foreign policy initiatives that provided a complete contrast: the Marshall Plan in the late 1940s and the ending of the Cuban missile crisis, which had threatened a new world war in 1962. He showed how the difference had been that these initiatives were driven by the very opposite of groupthink. In each case, those responsible had deliberately canvassed the widest range of expert opinion, to ensure that all relevant evidence was brought to the table. They wanted to explore every possible consequence of what was being proposed. And in each case the policy was outstandingly successful.

Once we recognise how these three elements make up the archetypal rules that define the operations of groupthink, we see just how very much more generally they have applied, in different guises, all down the ages.

An obvious example comes in the shape of most forms of organised religion. Religions are, by definition, 'belief systems', which, once established, have tended to become very markedly intolerant of anyone who does not share them. These outsiders are therefore condemned as 'heretics', 'infidels', and 'unbelievers'. To protect the right-thinking orthodoxy, they have to be marginalised, excluded from mainstream society, persecuted, even put to death.

Another obvious instance has been those totalitarian political ideologies, such as communism or Nazism, that likewise showed ruthless intolerance towards 'subversives', 'dissidents' or anyone not following 'the party line' (in the Soviet Union it was termed 'correct thinking'). Again, such people had to be excluded from established society, imprisoned or physically 'eliminated'.

Once we recognise this pattern, we can easily identify countless other examples, large and small, throughout history; from the treatment accorded to Galileo for questioning the Church's 'consensus' that the sun moved round the earth to the hysteria whipped up in the USA in the early1950s by McCarthy and the Senate Un-American Activities Committee, against anyone who could be demonised as a 'communist' and therefore a traitor.

A perfect fictional depiction of groupthink in action is Hans Christian Andersen's story *The Emperor's New Clothes*. When the emperor parades through the streets in what he has been talked into imagining is a dazzling new suit, all his deferential subjects acclaim it as handsome beyond compare. Only the little boy points out that the emperor is not wearing any clothes at all, and is stark naked. And, of course, those caught up in the 'consensus' all viciously turn on him for pointing out the truth.

In the epilogue I shall refer briefly to other instances of groupthink that have become only too familiar in our present-day world. But before we apply Janis's three rules to the 'non-debate' over global warming, we must also add one more very important aspect of the way groupthink operates which he didn't touch on, because it wasn't relevant to the particular examples he was analysing.

4 The power of second-hand thinking

> Great power is given to ideas propagated by affirmation, repetition and contagion by the circumstances that they acquire in time that mysterious force known as 'prestige'. Whatever has been a ruling power in the world, whether it be ideas or men, has in the main enforced its authority by means of that irresistible force we call prestige.
>
> Gustave Le Bon, *The Crowd*

Janis was only really concerned with how groupthink affected small groups of people in charge of US policy at the highest level. But when we come to consider the story of the belief in man-made global warming, we are of course looking at how this was shared by countless other people: academics, politicians, the media, teachers, business executives, indeed public opinion in general.

But all these people only got carried along by the belief that manmade global warming was real and dangerous because they had been told it was so by others. They accepted as true what they had heard, read or just seen on television without questioning it. And this meant that they didn't really know why they thought why they did. They hadn't thought it necessary to give such a complicated and technical subject any fundamental study. They simply echoed what had been passed on to them from somewhere else, usually in the form of a few familiar arguments or articles of belief that were, like approved mantras, endlessly repeated.

Of course, we all accept a huge proportion of what we believe or think we know without bothering to check the reliability of whatever source we first learned it from, such as the idea that the Earth is 93 million miles from the Sun, or that Tokyo is the capital of Japan. We just take on trust that such things are true because everyone else does so, and assume that, if necessary, they can be confirmed by hard evidence.

But when it came to the belief in man-made global warming, another factor was at work, one which always becomes relevant when we are looking at any case of groupthink. Because this was a wholly new idea, its acceptance rested on how much authority could be attributed to those putting it forward, and this was to become a crucial part of the story.

Long before Janis came up with his theory of groupthink, similar ideas had been explored in less scientific form by the French writer Gustave Le Bon, who in 1895 published a book called *The Crowd*. And one of his shrewdest observations was the crucial part played in changing the opinions of huge numbers of people by 'prestige': the particular deference paid to those who are taking the lead in putting them forward.

This was never more evident than in the way the belief in manmade global warming came to win such widespread acceptance. The most obvious example was the unique prestige accorded to the body known as the UN Intergovernmental Panel on Climate Change (IPCC). The prestige of the IPCC lay in the fact that it was presented to the world as the ultimate objective authority on the state of the earth's climate, representing the views of all the world's 'top climate scientists'. If other scientists, politicians, journalists or anyone else wished to make a point about global warming, they only had to cite the IPCC as their authority. Its pronouncements were to be treated as gospel. And even these people borrowed a little of the IPCC's authority by the very fact that they were quoting it.

But how did the IPCC come to be given such unparalleled authority in the first place? This becomes highly relevant when we look at how closely the rise of the belief in global warming and all that followed from it was shaped by Janis's three basic rules.

5 Global warming and the archetype of groupthink

We start by re-examining how the belief in man-made global warming first came about.

Rule 1: The creation of a belief-system

One of the most striking features of this belief was the dramatic suddenness with which it was sprung upon the world. The story began in obscurity in the late 1970s, when a tiny group of international meteorologists, led by Professor Bert Bolin from Sweden, observed that global temperatures, after 30 years of modest decline, were once again rising. In fact, Bolin had initially become convinced as far back as the late 1950s that a rise in carbon dioxide must inevitably, thanks to the properties of carbon dioxide as a greenhouse gas, lead to global warming, at a time when such a theory was wholly out of fashion. By the early 1970s, after three decades when global temperatures had been in such decline that many scientists were predicting the approach of a new ice age, Bolin was regarded as just an eccentrically marginal figure.[2]

But by the late 1970s, he noted that not only were levels of carbon dioxide rising, so also once again were temperatures. This confirmed for him that the two must be directly connected, the first leading to the second. And the possible consequences for the future of mankind, he concluded, were distinctly alarming.[3]

When, in 1979, Bolin put his case to the first ever 'World Climate Conference', staged in Geneva under the auspices of the World Meteorological Organization (the WMO), it seemed to his audience so convincing that it was agreed that a further conference should be held, at which Bolin's theory would be top of the agenda.

When another meeting took place at Villach, Austria, in 1985, Bolin had prepared a long paper, arguing that the problem of 'human-induced climate change' was potentially so serious that it called for urgent global action at the highest level. The conference endorsed all that Bolin said, and among those who found it particularly powerful was Dr John Houghton, an evangelical Christian who had formerly been professor of atmospheric physics at Oxford, but who since 1983 had been the head of the UK Met Office. He was now to become Bolin's most influential scientific ally.

But they might still have got nowhere with their cause had they not won an even more influential political ally, a very rich but strongly left-wing Canadian businessman, Maurice Strong. Since his teens, Strong had become convinced that the future of mankind lay in transforming the UN into a world government. He had also become a very skilful political networker at the highest level. In 1972, thanks to his personal links with the head of the UN, he had been appointed to organise in Stockholm a 'world conference on the environment'; and this led him to being asked to set up, as its first head, a new UN agency, the UN Environment Program (UNEP).

In fact, Strong knew very little about the environment. But he had now come to see it as the key to using the UN's prestige to promote a sweeping left-wing agenda. He argued that the natural resources of the earth were the common inheritance of all mankind, and that the rich Western countries, which had benefited so disproportionately from exploiting them, must now be made to fund the poorer countries in the rest of the world, to help their economies to catch up.

In 1985, although Strong had by then stepped down as its director, it was UNEP which joined the WMO in sponsoring the Villach climate conference. The meeting was chaired by Strong's like-minded successor as head of UNEP, Dr Mustafa Tolba. In 1987 the two men were able to push their agenda significantly further as members of the Brundtland Commission, the body that was to put the word 'sustainable' into the jargon of politicians and officialdom for decades to come. Thanks to their evidence and citing the recommendations from Villach, the Brundtland report laid particular emphasis on the dangers of 'human-induced climate change', warning that this could raise global temperatures to such a level that it would have serious effects on agriculture, 'raise sea levels, flood coastal cities and disrupt national economies'. The report therefore called for a major global effort to curb emissions of carbon dioxide and other greenhouse gases.

In the same year, Strong played a key behind-the-scenes role in organising the conference in his native Canada that produced the Montreal Protocol, the first global treaty to 'protect the environment', that succeeded in phasing out the use of CFCs, the chemicals thought to be destroying the ozone layer. This process enabled Strong to see that, in global warming, he had found an even more powerful theme on which to push his long-time political agenda. And in the landmark year of 1988 everything seemed suddenly to be coming together.

First, on a stiflingly hot July day in Washington that summer, a Senate committee heard a cleverly stage-managed rallying cry by another recent convert to the global warming cause, James Hansen, who, as head of NASA's Goddard Institute for Space Studies (GISS), was in charge of one of the world's key official temperature records. The US media had been briefed to be present in force at this hearing, chaired by Senator Tim Wirth and including among the members of its committee, Senator Al Gore. The journalists were promised that they would hear something pretty sensational. Hansen's wildly alarmist predictions that the world was heading for a global Armageddon duly made lurid headlines across USA and beyond, including cover stories in *Time* and *Newsweek*. Wirth and Hansen had certainly pulled off quite a coup in raising the threat of global warming to the top of the media agenda.

Quite separately, however, in November that year in Geneva, took place the inaugural meeting of a new body, jointly sponsored by WMO and UNEP: the IPCC. Although it was to be sold to the world as an impartial body of world scientists, the IPCC was never intended by those who set it up to be anything of the kind. The two men more than any responsible for this were Bolin, appointed as its first chairman, and Houghton, chosen to chair 'Working Group I', which would contribute the all-important section on the science of climate change when the IPCC came to compile its first report. Not only were both men totally committed to the belief in 'human induced climate change', so were almost all the lesser mortals round the table at that first IPCC meeting, representing 34 nations, as can be seen from the statements each submitted on behalf of their respective governments.[4] Within just two years, it was proposed, the IPCC would present its first 'assessment report', in which the key ingredient would be computer models programmed to determine the extent to which rising levels of carbon dioxide would warm the world.[5]

When this First Assessment Report appeared in 1990, the global headlines were led by a claim in its 'Summary for Policymakers' that the IPCC was 'confident that the increase in CO_2 alone' had been responsible for 'more than half the world's recent warming' and that this would 'require immediate reductions in emissions from human activities of over 60 percent'.

'Based on current models', the Summary predicted that, unless drastic action was taken, global temperatures would increase through the 21st century by up to 0.5°C every decade, an increase far greater than anything 'seen in the past 10,000 years'. Although in the previous 100 years temperatures had increased by 0.6°C, the models were now predicting the possibility of a not dissimilar increase every ten years. But the Summary for Policymakers was drafted by Houghton himself. And a look at the hundreds of pages which it was purporting to summarise showed a rather different picture. Some of the scientists responsible for them had come to very much more cautious, if not contradictory conclusions. One passage, for instance, admitted that:

> ...global warming of a larger size has almost certainly occurred at least once since the last glaciation without any appreciable increase in greenhouse gases... [and] because we do not understand the reasons for these past warming events, it is not possible to attribute a specific proportion of the recent, smaller warming to an increase in greenhouse gases.

But it was Houghton's alarmist gloss on the actual findings of the report that, as was intended, caught the attention of the world's media and politicians. And this was just what was wanted by their ally Strong, who was even now preparing for the unprecedented spectacular he planned to stage in Rio de Janeiro two years later.

The so-called 'Earth Summit', which Strong organised and chaired in Rio in 1992, was easily the largest conference the world had ever seen. It was attended by 108 world leaders, ranging from Cuba's Fidel Castro to a rather more reluctant US President George Bush Sr, along with 20,000 other official delegates. Also present in Rio were 20,000 climate activists and members of green lobby groups, all paid for out of UN and government funds, as arranged by Strong himself. He masterminded every detail of this extraordinary gathering, and ensured that it would set up a Framework Convention on Climate Change (UNFCCC) to guide the advance to a global 'climate policy'.

It was planned that in 1997 the UNFCCC would stage another mega-conference in Kyoto, where the nations of the world would sign a treaty agreeing to make drastic cuts in carbon dioxide emissions. Or, to be more precise, in accordance with Strong's real long-term agenda, this treaty would commit the 'developed' countries of the West to reduce their carbon dioxide emissions (since they were considered chiefly responsible for the problem), while paying out huge sums to the still-developing nations in the rest of the world, including China and India, to assist their economies to catch up with the West.

For the tiny handful of meteorologists who, in the mid-1980s, had been discussing how to get politicians to accept that global warming was a serious threat, all this amounted to an amazing coup. In just four short years they had raised it to the top of the world's political agenda. The first world leader to come on board in 1988 had been Britain's prime minister, Margaret Thatcher, who had been converted to the cause by the UK's ambassador to the UN, Crispin Tickell. He had won her over not least by citing Hansen's evidence to the Senate committee. And she had then given enthusiastic backing to John Houghton in his plans to set up the IPCC, and the funding to create a new department of his UK Met Office, the Hadley Centre for Climate Change (later to become the Hadley Centre for Climate Prediction and Research). This would be responsible, with the Climatic Research Unit (CRU) of the University of East Anglia, for another of what became the world's four main global temperature records.[6]

In America, the most prominent politician now totally committed to the cause was Senator Al Gore from Tennessee; a member of that Senate committee in 1988, who was about to become US vice-president under Bill Clinton.

In Brussels in October 1991, the European Community (shortly to become the European Union) had acclaimed the IPCC report for showing how, for the first time, there was now 'a consensus among scientists on the possible impact and risks of the greenhouse effect'. This came in a long document setting out *A Community Strategy to Limit Carbon Dioxide Emissions*, proposing a Europe-wide conversion to renewable energy.

All in all, it was clear that the need to 'combat climate change' was very much an idea whose time had come. But in light of the first step in Janis's three-stage analysis, we must note that, even then, the scientific base for the theory of the 'true believers' was in no way as secure as they pretended. The only 'proof' that they were right lay in the projections of those computer models, specifically programmed to assume that rising carbon dioxide was the most important factor driving global temperatures and therefore changes to the climate. Politically, they had certainly made astonishing progress. But, as was shown by the way Houghton had needed to 'sex up' his Summary for Policymakers, they were still having to push pretty hard to make their case seem as watertight as they would have liked. And it was already becoming very evident that those who supported their cause were having to move on to the second stage of the Janis rules, by insisting whenever possible that the case for 'human-induced climate change' was now accepted by a 'consensus' of the world's scientists.

Rule 2: Creating the illusion of a 'consensus'

> Only an insignificant fraction of scientists deny the global warming crisis. The time for debate is over. The science is settled.
>
> Al Gore, 1992

One eminent scientist very much not part of the 'consensus' was Dr Richard Lindzen, the Alfred P. Sloan Professor of Meteorology at the Massachusetts Institute of Technology and one of America's most respected atmospheric physicists. In 1992 he published a long informal paper entitled 'Global warming: the origin and nature of the alleged scientific consensus', the theme of which was the extraordinary pressure that had built up in the late 1980s to create the impression that global warming was supported by an overwhelming 'consensus' of scientific opinion. He began by recalling a letter he had received in 1988 from a respected professor of economics named Lester Lave, who had been one of the other witnesses called before the 1988 Senate committee at which James Hansen had spoken so dramatically.

Unlike Hansen, Lave had told the senators that the global warming hypothesis was still 'controversial', that by no means all scientists were agreed on it, and that the science was still very uncertain as to what the causes of climate change might be. Senator Gore expressed vehement irritation at this, claiming that anyone who said such a thing couldn't know what he was talking about, and suggesting that there was no point in the senators hearing any more of Professor Lave's evidence.[7]

Lave had been so surprised to be dismissed by the committee in such summary fashion that he had written to Lindzen, as one of America's most distinguished climatologists, to ask whether he had got it wrong. Lindzen confirmed that the case for global warming was not only 'controversial' but also, in his view, 'implausible'.[8]

Two years later, when the IPCC produced its first report, as Lindzen described, he had found it as a scientist deeply disturbing. He too had been shocked by the way Houghton's Summary for Policymakers had largely ignored the 'uncertainty' expressed in parts of the report itself, by attempting 'to present the expectation of substantial warming as firmly based science'.[9] Indeed this had essentially been confirmed by Houghton himself, admitting that:

> ...whilst every attempt was made by the lead authors to incorporate their comments, in some cases these formed a minority opinion which could not be reconciled with the larger consensus.[10]

But Lindzen's chief objections to the report were based on the area of science in which he himself had unrivalled expertise. He noted that the IPCC's predictions of future temperatures and climate behaviour were all based on computer models. And what particularly struck him was that the programming of these models was much too simplistic. By giving pole position to carbon dioxide and other greenhouse gases as the main 'forcing' ingredient in driving future temperatures, and by failing to allow for other natural influences on climate, their findings were demonstrably misleading.

In particular, observed Lindzen, models overlooked or seriously misjudged the part played by far the most important greenhouse gas of all, water vapour, which makes up more than 90 percent of their total volume. They also failed to allow for the effect of the increased cloud-cover that would result from the greater humidity caused by warming of the oceans. Each of these effects would lessen the impact of global warming. Account for them properly in the models, he argued, and it would be seen that the 'greenhouse effect' caused by rising carbon dioxide levels had been wildly overstated. What was more, this could be demonstrated by running those same computer models retrospectively, to show where, if they were right, temperatures should have been throughout the 20th century. It became glaringly obvious that these crudely over-simplified programmes failed to explain the actual variations that had taken place in 20th century temperature levels. In the 1920s and 1930s, when carbon dioxide emissions were comparatively low, temperatures had sharply risen. But in the very years when emissions were rising much more steeply, between 1940 and the 1970s, temperatures had fallen back, in what became known to climatologists as the 'Little Cooling'. In fact, the assumptions on which the models were based, said Lindzen, would have led them to predict a 20th century warming four times greater than that actually recorded (with most of the rise taking place before atmospheric carbon dioxide had reached anything like its present level). On this basis, how could any trust now be placed in their pretended ability to estimate future rises? As Lindzen bluntly put it, the models had 'neither the physics nor the numerical accuracy to come up with findings which were not 'disturbingly arbitrary'.

But even though this confirmed why Lindzen found the IPCC's case for future warming 'implausible' and seriously exaggerated, his lengthy paper on the nature of the supposed 'consensus' in fact ranged very much wider. In particular, he focussed on both the remarkable degree to which the notion of a 'consensus' had been used to dominate public debate and also the extraordinary pressure brought to bear to ensure that anyone daring to question it was marginalised.

For a start, it had been notable how quickly other influential interest groups had rushed to join the cause. He described, for instance, how fervently global warming had been taken up by the leading environmental campaigning organisations, such as Greenpeace, Friends of the Earth and the WWF. These pressure groups, which had originally emerged out of the 'environmental awakening' of the 1960s, had now attained very considerable status and influence as 'non-governmental organisations' (NGOs).

The chief original target of all these campaigning groups had been the need to save the world from the 'threat' posed by nuclear weapons and nuclear power stations.[11] But with remarkable unanimity, as the Cold War came to an end, they had all suddenly switched the focus of their attention to this new threat to the planet. As Lindzen put it:

> ...these lobbying groups have budgets of several million dollars and employ about 50,000 people. Their support is highly valued by many political figures. As with any large groups, self-perpetuation becomes a crucial concern. 'Global warming' has become one of the major battle cries in their fundraising efforts. At the same time, the media unquestioningly accept the pronouncements of these groups as objective truth.

In March 1989 the main NGOs had formed an umbrella organisation, the Climate Action Network, to co-ordinate their campaigning on global warming. This shadowy body was to be used by Strong in 1992 to co-ordinate his recruiting of the 20,000 activists who attended his Rio summit.

At the same time, another such group, the Union of Concerned Scientists, which had also originally been formed to campaign on nuclear issues, organised a petition urging the recognition of global warming as potentially the greatest danger faced by mankind. The eventual list of 700 signatories, including Nobel prizewinners and many members of the National Academy of Sciences, seemed hugely impressive. But 'only about three or four' of them, according to Lindzen, were qualified climate scientists.

At the 1990 meeting of the National Academy, its president, referring specifically to this petition, went out of his way to warn members against 'lending their credibility to issues about which they had no special knowledge'.[12] His warning was to be conspicuously ignored.

Lindzen also recalled how quickly the new cause had become fashionable among leading figures in showbusiness, such as the Hollywood actors Robert Redford, Barbra Streisand and Meryl Streep, all of whom made much-publicised calls, in Redford's words, for people to stop just 'researching' the warming threat and to 'begin acting' (which, as Lindzen wryly observed, was not an unreasonable thing for an actor to suggest).

Also now becoming obvious, however, was just how much new money was now becoming available for research into climate change. Even though in 1989 President George Bush Sr's senior White House advisers had initially been sceptical on the issue, so great now was political pressure that in 1989 they authorised a staggering increase in the federal budget for climate change research. Over the next four years this was to increase from just $134 million to a total of $2.8 billion.[13]

But, as Lindzen noted, it had soon become clear that any proposals deemed likely to be at all ambivalent over global warming were highly unlikely to be accepted. He recalled how, in the winter of 1989, the National Science Foundation had withdrawn funding from one of his MIT colleagues, Professor Reginald Newell, when his data analyses failed to show that the previous century had seen a net warming (one reviewer suggested that his results were 'dangerous to humanity').[14]

This was an indication of just how ruthless the pressure had become to shut any critics of the 'consensus' out of the debate. When Lindzen himself submitted a critique of the global warming thesis to *Science*, the journal of the American Association for the Advancement of Science, his article was rejected as being of 'no interest' to its readership. But, to his astonishment, *Science* then proceeded to attack his paper even though it had not been published.

Although the article eventually appeared in the *Bulletin of the American Meteorological Society*, its editor made 'a determined effort to solicit rebuttals', including one that was an attack on Lindzen by Stephen Schneider, a scientist who in the 1970s had been a prominent supporter of the belief that the world might be heading for a new ice age, but was now one of the leading advocates of warming.

The letters the paper aroused from the *Bulletin's* readers, however, were predominantly sceptical of the case for anthropogenic warming. Indeed, a subsequent Gallup poll of climate scientists belonging to the American Meteorological Society and the American Physical Union showed that no fewer than 49 percent rejected it. Only 18 percent thought that some warming was caused by man, while 33 percent were 'don't knows'.

Lindzen noted how a number of the scientists participating in the IPCC report had

> ...testified to the pressure put on them to emphasise results supportive of the current scenario and to suppress other results. That pressure has frequently been effective, and a survey of participants reveals substantial disagreement with the final report.[15]

'Why, one might wonder', Lindzen asked, was 'there such insistence on scientific unanimity on the warming issue'? After all, he observed,

> ...unanimity in science is virtually non-existent on far less complex matters. Unanimity on an issue as uncertain as 'global warming' would be surprising and suspicious. Moreover, why are the opinions of scientists sought regardless of their field of expertise? Biologists and physicians are rarely asked to endorse some theory in high-energy physics. Apparently, when one comes to 'global warming', any scientist's agreement will do.

The supporters of the 'consensus' were now clearly becoming impatient of anyone who dared question their orthodoxy. This takes us on to the final stage of Janis's three rules of groupthink:

the ruthless way in which a 'consensus' must be defended against anyone who disagrees with it. This is necessary for upholders of the 'consensus', not only in propaganda terms, showing a wider audience how any critics can safely be ignored, but in psychological terms, by reinforcing their own belief that the 'consensus' is unquestionably right.

Rule 3: Putting 'non-believers' beyond the pale

Once Lindzen's sceptical views had become known, as he described in his paper, he had been singled out for venomous attack, even in books, such as *World on Fire: Saving an Endangered Earth*, published in 1991 by George Mitchell, the Democrats' majority leader in the Senate. In fact Lindzen was far from alone in being given such treatment. He and other 'climate sceptics' were now being regularly subjected to dismissive ridicule in the press, as in an article in the *New York Times* by Al Gore, in which, by somewhat ironic projection, he compared those who shared his views to Galileo, bravely standing for the truth against the intolerant consensus of his time.

But just how vicious in suppressing criticism the supporters of the 'consensus' had become was illustrated by the fate of two other eminent scientists who had also publicly shown that they did not subscribe to the 'consensus'. In the summer of 1992, Al Gore, by now the leading political crusader on global warming in America, was bidding to become the Democrat Party's candidate for vice-president. As part of his campaign he published a book, *Earth in the Balance*, claiming that global warming was 'the worst threat we have ever faced'.[16]

Gore paid glowing tribute to the man who had first alerted him to this threat when he was at Harvard in the mid-1960s: the distinguished oceanographer, Roger Revelle. Back in the 1950s, as head of a department at the University of California in San Diego, Revelle had been behind the setting up of the research station on top of the Hawaiian volcano Mauna Loa that measures the levels of carbon dioxide in the atmosphere. When the data had shown that these were steadily rising, it was this more than anything else that helped to set the great alarm over global warming on its way.

When Gore wrote his book in 1992, he seemed unaware that, although Revelle had recognised a possible connection between greenhouse gases and global temperatures, he had long been taking a very much more cautious view on global warming than that now being championed by Gore himself. In July 1988, after Hansen made headlines with his testimony to Wirth's Senate committee, Revelle had written to a member of Congress:

> Most scientists familiar with the subject are not yet willing to bet that the climate this year is the result of 'greenhouse warming'. As you very well know, climate is highly variable from year to year, and the causes of these variations are not at all well understood. My own personal belief is that we should wait another ten or twenty years to really be convinced that the greenhouse effect is going to be important for human beings, in both positive and negative ways.[17]

Four days later Revelle had written to Wirth himself, cautioning that:

> ...we should be careful not to arouse too much alarm until the rate and amount of warming becomes clearer. It is not yet obvious that this summer's hot weather and drought are the result of a global climatic change or simply an example of the uncertainties of climate vari-

> ability. My own feeling is that we had better wait another ten years before making confident predictions.[18]

In 1990, at a conference of the American Association for the Advancement of Science, Revelle was approached by an old friend, Dr Fred Singer, then professor of environmental science at the University of Virginia, but who, back in the 1960s, had worked with NASA to design and set up, as its first director, the US National Satellite Weather Service. The two men discussed writing an informal paper together on global warming, which Singer went on to draft for submission to a small-circulation journal called *Cosmos*. When he and Revelle met to discuss the proofs, they agreed several amendments, and the article was published in April 1991. It was entitled 'What to do about greenhouse warming: look before you leap'. Their main argument, echoing the views that Revelle had expressed earlier in his letters to the members of Congress, was that:

> Drastic, precipitous, and especially unilateral steps to delay the putative greenhouse impacts can cost jobs and prosperity and increase the human costs of global poverty without being effective. Stringent economic controls now would be economically devastating particularly for developing countries...'

They concluded that:

> ...the scientific base for a greenhouse warming is too uncertain to justify drastic action at this time.

The article attracted little attention and three months later, professionally active to the end of his life, Revelle died aged 82. Later that year, however, Singer was invited to contribute to a book on global warming and suggested that their article be republished.

The following summer of 1992, when Al Gore was running hard to win the vice-presidential nomination, the *New Republic* picked up on the contrast between the references to Revelle in his new book and the views expressed in the article he had co-authored with Singer.[19] This was prominently reported elsewhere in the media and, after Gore won the nomination, was even raised in a televised election debate. Gore's response was not only to protest that Revelle's views in the article had been 'taken completely out of context', but to use one of his close associates, Dr Justin Lancaster of Harvard, to ask Singer to remove Revelle's name from the article. This was somewhat impractical, since it had already been published.

However, Lancaster persisted in his efforts, not only claiming that Revelle had not really been a co-author of the article and that his name had only been included 'over his objections', but even suggesting that Singer must have been pressuring a sick old man whose mental capacities were failing.

When, after Gore had become US vice-president, Lancaster repeated his charges, Singer in April 1993 sued him for libel. And this led to a remarkable revelation. When the two sides exchanged documents, it emerged that it was Gore who had particularly pressed Lancaster about Revelle's mental state towards the end of his life: hence Lancaster's suggestions that Singer had been quite improperly exploiting Revelle's loss of his faculties.

But Lancaster was now prepared to agree that Revelle had in fact been 'mentally sharp to the end'. He also admitted that Revelle had shown him the article before it was published, with the comment that there did not seem to be anything in it that 'was not true'.[20]

In February 1994, an ABC News presenter, Ted Koppel, revealed on his *Nightline* programme that Vice President Gore had rung him in person, suggesting that he should expose the sinister political and economic forces behind what he called the 'anti-environmental movement'. Gore had in particular urged him to expose the fact that Singer and other scientists who had voiced sceptical views about global warming were receiving money from the coal industry and other fossil-fuel interests.

Such charges were already becoming an all-too familiar feature of the debate. Anyone daring to express doubts about the 'consensus' might now face accusations that they could only be expressing these views because they had been paid to do so by energy firms, 'Big Oil' or even the tobacco industry.[21] But when Koppel called Gore's bluff by reporting the call from the vice-president on air, this attempt to use a leading news programme to discredit his opponents provoked such political embarrassment that, shortly afterwards, Lancaster settled his case with Singer by issuing a full retraction and apology.[22]

This sorry episode was a further graphic illustration of how those caught up in any form of groupthink are likely to respond to anyone who doesn't agree with them. As Janis showed, because the only evidence they are willing to recognise is that which confirms their own mindset, anyone who dissents must be discredited, stereotyped and caricatured as only doing so from some ignoble motive.

Rather than attempting to address the points dissenters are raising, these are routinely countered by ad-hominem attacks on their character. Some dark reason must be found to explain why such people should not be listened to, such as suggesting that they are only questioning the 'consensus' because they are being paid to do so.

But such propaganda tactics can only be effective so long as the illusory 'consensus' continues to hold the moral high ground.

6 The 'idea whose time had come'

> In searching for a new enemy to unite us, we came up with the idea that pollution, the threat of global warming, water shortages, famine and the like would fit the bill...all these dangers are caused by human intervention...the real enemy then is humanity itself.
>
> *The First Global Revolution*, Report by the Club of Rome, 1991[23]

So far, we have looked in some detail at how the origins of this belief system provide a perfect case study in the workings of groupthink, by demonstrating how all the three stages of this archetypal pattern so quickly emerged from the very start of the global warming story. We shall shortly follow that story in a more summary form, looking at just some of the more conspicuous examples of how consistently Janis's rules continued to shape it over the years to come. But first we must briefly consider two of the deeper psychological reasons why the global warming 'narrative' had so widely and rapidly taken hold in the late 1980s, as an 'idea whose time had come'.

The first reason was the profound shift in collective consciousness that had taken place in the late 1950s and 1960s, giving rise to what became known as 'environmentalism' and the 'environmental movement'. This was the awareness that, for the first time in history, science had given mankind the power to destroy all life on earth. Obviously, the supreme expression of this idea was the fearful shadow cast by the possibility of nuclear war. With the Cold War, the world was divided between two great camps, each armed with missiles carrying hydrogen bombs, capable not just of immediate catastrophic destruction but of spreading radioactivity so widely that it might render large parts of the planet uninhabitable.

But this realisation also coincided with a new awareness of the damage mankind was already inflicting on nature and the natural environment, through toxic chemicals, the methods of modern agriculture, the ever-growing pollution of the seas by indestructible plastic wastes, the pressures of over-population and the evidence that so many species seemed now to be threatened by human activity with extinction.

In 1958 these fears had had given rise to the Campaign for Nuclear Disarmament, in 1961 to the founding of WWF and in 1962 to Rachel Carson's hugely best-selling *Silent Spring* on the threat posed to wildlife by pesticides. By the end of the 1960s it had led to the launching of the two most influential of all environmental campaigning groups, Greenpeace and Friends of the Earth, both initially focused on the nuclear threat.

No image caught the new mood of the time better than 'Earthrise', the picture of the soft blue Earth taken in 1968 from the Apollo 11 space mission, widely interpreted as showing how vulnerable the earth had become to the destructive powers of humanity as 'the only planet we've got'.

In 1972 came that first 'World Environment Conference', organised for the UN and shaped according to his own political agenda by Maurice Strong. In the same year, the Club of Rome's *The Limits to Growth* report, selling 37 million copies worldwide, used a computer model to show how population growth would soon outrun food production and natural resources, to threaten the survival of civilisation.

All this had created a mindset and a narrative which, by casting humanity as its own worst enemy, as 'the cuckoo in the nest of creation', was perfectly fitted by the late 1980s to take on board this great new scare story: that, quite apart from all the other threats mankind was posing to the future of the planet, conceivably the worst (apart of course from a nuclear holocaust) was the possibility that runaway global warming created by human emissions of greenhouse gases might lead to the destruction of all life on earth.

This was why, as the Cold War came to an end, with the sudden collapse of the Soviet communist empire removing the fear of nuclear war almost overnight, those environmental groups that had been founded on their opposition to nuclear weapons and nuclear power, were able to morph seamlessly into seeing the need to fight the threat of man-made global warming as their new great cause. They were also joined in this by WWF, on the grounds that global warming was a serious new addition to its prime purpose, to fight for species threatened with extinction.

The key to the success of the new cause was precisely that it made such an appeal to the moral sense. Those caught up in it were convinced that they were supporting the 'good guys' in wanting to 'save the planet' from a quite unprecedented catastrophe. But they were thus fitting into a very ancient and archetypal pattern of collective human psychology. Ever since the biblical story of Noah, history (or myth) had been full of episodes where it was believed that mankind was facing some immense disaster that threatened the end of the world. Common to all such millennial scenarios was the conviction that this would be a punishment for the wickedness of the human race in having taken a morally wrong turning. And a very powerful part of the appeal of this particular narrative was that it divided the world into the 'bad guys' who had set humanity on course for disaster by persuading it down the primrose path of dependence on those evil fossil fuels, and the 'good guys' who had finally woken up to how dangerously mistaken this had been. By joining this new holy cause, one was choosing to side with 'life' rather than continuing blindly on a course which would otherwise bring death to all life on earth - unless humanity could be persuaded to wake up in time, and to take the very drastic actions that alone could bring salvation.

If any form of groupthink relies on a conviction that it holds the moral high ground, the 'consensus' over global warming was about to face its own first real moral challenge. This was when, for the first time, a serious scandal came to light over the inner workings of its most prestigious authority, the IPCC.

7 The IPCC breaks its own rules: the 'consensus' survives its first major scandal

> The members' firm belief in the morality of their group and their use of undifferentiated stereotypes of their opponents would enable them to minimise conflicts between ethical values and expediency... 'Since our group's objectives are good', the members feel, 'any means we decide to use must be good'... Shared negative stereotypes that feature the evil nature of the enemy would enhance their sense of moral righteousness and their pride in the lofty mission of the in-group.
>
> Irving Janis, *Groupthink*

> If the IPCC is incapable of following its most basic procedures, it would be best to abandon the entire IPCC process, or at least that part that is concerned with the scientific evidence on climate change, and look for more reliable sources of advice on this important question.
>
> Professor Frederick Seitz, former President of the National Academy of Sciences[24]

The scandal erupted in 1996, following the publication of the IPCC's Second Assessment Report, although on this occasion it had been decided to issue the Summary for Policymakers some time before the release of the full report. One sentence in it had caught worldwide headlines. It claimed that 'the balance of evidence suggests that there is a discernible human influence on global climate'. And the source for this was given as Chapter 8 of the Working Group 1 report. Sure enough, when the full report did finally appear, a similar sentence was discovered buried away in its hundreds of pages.

But no one was more surprised by this than several of the scientific contributors to those same pages, who had earlier signed off the text as an accurate record of what they had agreed. These now much-quoted words had not appeared in the draft they formally approved at a meeting in Madrid in November 1995 (also attended by 177 government delegates from 96 countries and 14 NGO representatives).[25] Particularly odd was that the only sources cited for the new wording were two papers co-authored by one of the lead authors on this part of the report: a scientist employed by the US government named Ben Santer. In clear breach of one of the IPCC's strictest rules, these two cited papers had not even yet been published.

What astonished the scientists even more, however, was to discover that no less than 15 key statements from their agreed text had been deleted. And each of these had expressed serious doubt over the human contribution to global warming. They included, for instance, such statements as:

> None of the studies cited above has shown clear evidence that we can attribute the observed changes to the specific cause of increases in greenhouse gases.

and

> No study to date has positively attributed all or part (of the climate change observed) to (man-made) causes.

This all seemed so irregular that, a week after the full report appeared, the *Wall Street Journal* published a devastating article headed 'Major deception on global warming', by one of the most respected scientists in America, Professor Frederick Seitz, a former president of the National Academy of Sciences.[26] Seitz quoted some of the 15 passages that had been so damningly deleted, thundering that:

> In my more than 60 years as a member of the American scientific community, including service as president of both the National Academy of Sciences and the American Physical Society, I have never witnessed a more disturbing corruption of the peer-review process than the events which led up to this IPCC report.

'The major responsibility' for what had happened, he suggested, must lie with the lead author, Santer. 'IPCC reports', Seitz observed, 'are often called the "consensus" view'. But if they were to lead to 'carbon taxes and restraints on economic growth, they will have a major and almost certainly destructive effect on the economies of the world'. He went on

> Whatever the intent was of those who made these significant changes, their effect is to deceive policy makers and the public into believing that scientific evidence shows human activities are causing global warming.

The IPCC establishment was clearly very shaken at having been caught out like this. So unimpeachable was Seitz's reputation that his article could not simply be ignored. Nor was it possible to discredit him personally (although that limp effort was made to associate him with Fred Singer, as co-authors of a paper which, it was insinuated, must have been funded by allies of the tobacco industry).

The *Wall Street Journal* published defensive letters from both Bolin and Houghton, along with one from Santer himself, (co-signed by Tom Wigley, another close adviser of Al Gore and former director of the University of East Anglia's CRU), all denying that what had happened had been in breach of the IPCC's rules.

This point was developed in a paper by another member of the IPCC establishment, Stephen Schneider, who had also been present at the Madrid meeting.[27] He did confirm that it was Santer who had been responsible for all the deletions and additions. But he also described how, entirely within the rules (as he claimed), a little group of scientists had then gone off into a separate room to approve the changes.[28] What only came to light two years later, in evidence to a Congressional committee, was the sequence of events that had preceded the making of the changes. Before the contributing scientists had signed off the text, Houghton, as the report's editor, received a message from the State Department in Washington, which read:

> It is essential that the chapters not be finalised prior to the completion of the discussions at the IPCC Working Group 1 Plenary in Madrid, and that chapter authors be prevailed upon to modify their text in an appropriate manner following the discussion in Madrid.[29]

This instruction had come from the office of the man who was now the US Under-Secretary of State for Global Affairs: Timothy Wirth, the longtime close ally of Vice President Gore and chairman of those historic Senate committee hearings in 1988. Top of the US administration's agenda at the time had been the effort to ensure a successful outcome to the global climate conference due to take place in Kyoto in 1997. For this they considered it vital that the IPCC should pronounce more forcefully than before that there could no longer be any doubt that global warming was caused by human activity.

By any measure, this episode might have led observers to question whether the IPCC was quite the impartial, non-political body it was purported to be. But such was the power of the groupthink, which now held so many in its grip – not least the media – that the dust soon settled. The authority of IPCC, as representing a 'consensus of the world's top climate scientists', emerged unscathed.

It is a fair guess that few of the 10,000 people who attended the UNFCCC's mega-conference in Kyoto in December 1997 were not (in every sense) fully paid-up supporters of the 'consensus'. They included 2000 official delegates – politicians, officials and academics – supported by 5000 fully-funded climate activists and members of green lobby groups (44 from Greenpeace alone), plus 3000 representatives of the world's media, almost all of whom would have been sympathetic to the conference's aims. The star of the show was Vice President Gore, who descended by helicopter on the main conference hotel just in time to give the opening keynote address. Also much in evidence, though no longer chairing the occasion, was Maurice Strong, And the purpose of the gathering was to sign the world's first full-scale global 'climate treaty' which, after months of fierce behind-the-scenes haggling, was very much on the lines originally drawn up by Strong.

The rich industrialised nations of the West, classified as 'Annex 1 countries', would agree to curb their carbon dioxide emissions, while the still 'developing' Annex 2 countries, including China and India, would be exempted, to allow their economies to catch up with the West. The one-sided nature of this deal put Gore on the spot, because it was precisely the reason why the US Senate had already voted 95-0 that America could not accept such a treaty. But, to unanimous applause, Gore signed it anyway.

Even though one of his close advisers, Tom Wigley, formerly director of the University of East Anglia's CRU, famously calculated that the emissions cuts signed up to by the developed countries would only slow the rise in global temperatures by six years, the political focus over the next few years was to persuade the requisite number of countries to ratify the treaty to bring it into force. And it had already been agreed that Kyoto was only a first step, to be replaced by another, much tougher treaty a few years down the line.

For all this, it was vital for the IPCC to step up the pressure with its next report, due in 2001. This was to lead to what would become, scientifically, the most revealing episode in its history.

8 The 'consensus' fudges the evidence

> He who controls the past, controls the future. He who controls the present, controls the past.
>
> George Orwell, *Nineteen Eighty-Four*

Up to now, it seemed the global warming theory was looking ever more plausible. As carbon dioxide levels continued to rise, so did the trend in global temperatures, seemingly just as predicted. But the one problem which more than anything worried the little group of scientists at the heart of the IPCC was the long-held assumption that during the Middle Ages – the so-called Medieval Warm Period – the world had been even hotter than it had become in the late-20th century. Obviously, this was centuries before it could have been blamed on man-made carbon dioxide.[30]

The story of how the IPCC got around this problem has long been familiar and fully documented.[31] It began in 1995 with a famous email from one of the little group of scientists at the heart of the IPCC, Jonathan Overpeck, to another scientist whom he assumed agreed with the 'consensus'. In it, Overpeck said 'we have to get rid of the Mediaeval Warm Period'.

Four years later, bang on cue, there appeared in *Nature* a graph, produced by a hitherto unknown young PhD, Michael Mann, which supplied just what was needed. Mann and two colleagues had wholly rewritten the accepted picture of historic world temperatures. Their graph showed temperatures having steadily declined over the past millennium in an almost unwavering downward line, until suddenly, in the late 20th century, they dramatically spiked upwards to by far their highest level in 1000 years (thus giving the graph the shape of the handle and blade of an ice-hockey stick). The Medieval Warm Period had completely disappeared. So had the four-centuries-long Little Ice Age. And it further helped that 1998 had been measured as the hottest year since modern temperature records began, bringing the graph to its suitably terrifying climax.

This was everything those at the top of the IPCC could have wanted. When its Third Assessment Report appeared in 2001, the 'hockey-stick' not only led the first page of the Summary for Policymakers but at the launch of the report, Houghton appeared to the media in front of a huge blow-up of Mann's graph. It also appeared five more times in the report itself. It was this startling image as much as anything that encouraged the Summary to go even further than its predecessors in claiming that 'there is new and stronger evidence that most of the warming observed over the past 50 years is attributable to human activity', and to predict that, within 100 years, global temperatures could have risen by as much as 5.8°C, much higher than anything suggested before.[32]

But it was also the strangely familiar hockey stick shape which, a year or two later, caught the attention of Steve McIntyre, a Canadian expert in statistics. As an industrial consultant, the shape of the hockey stick aroused his suspicion because he had often seen similar graphs produced by companies wishing to give an exaggeratedly optimistic picture of their future business prospects. When McIntyre and a Canadian economics professor, Ross McKitrick, used their expertise to analyse the way Mann had constructed the graph, they became increasingly astonished. In essence it seemed that Mann's algorithm was 'mining' the underlying data for hockey-stick shapes, and therefore would give a hockey stick result from whatever data was fed into it. In fact, although the graph purported to show temperatures over the past 1000 years for the whole of the Northern Hemisphere, Mann's initial 'proxy' temperature data had largely consisted just of tree-rings from North America (a notoriously unreliable way to measure past temperatures). But almost the only trees from the sample which actually had a hockey-stick shape had been one group of bristlecone pines in California.

Yet Mann's algorithm had given these 390 times more weight than a tree-ring sample from Arkansas which had failed to show a 'hockey stick' shape. Finally, and even more oddly, the temperatures for the closing decades of the 20th century were not based on tree-ring proxies at all. They were thermometer-recorded data, and in the much-publicised version of the graph published in the IPCC's 2001 report, they had been spliced onto the end of the tree-ring data.[33] It was only this combination of two wholly different data sources which gave the graph that final, eye-catching uptick.

Initially McIntyre and McKitrick had great difficulty in getting any scientific journal to publish their findings. *Nature*, which had originally published the graph and had long been a highly partisan advocate for the 'consensus', flatly refused to allow them to explain what their meticulous analysis had revealed.[34] But once they had found a journal willing to publish their findings, it became increasingly clear that the IPCC establishment had again been seriously caught out, and this time on the very 'evidence' it had made the single most widely publicised argument for their cause.

We later learned from the Climategate emails, leaked in 2009 from CRU, just what angst and anger this had aroused among that same intimately connected group of scientists who were now at the heart of the IPCC. In the exchanges of emails all their names were there: Mann himself, Ben Santer, Tom Wigley, Stephen Schneider, Jonathan Overpeck, Kevin Trenberth, and Gavin Schmidt, who was Hansen's number two at GISS and in charge of one of the two main global surface temperature records. At East Anglia itself, their close ally, CRU director Phil Jones, was responsible for the other surface record, HadCRUt.

What these emails also brought to light was that, just when Mann had been creating his 'hockey-stick', Jones's CRU colleague Keith Briffa had already been trying to produce a remarkably similar graph, also based on tree-ring 'proxies', this time from Siberia. But these had also frustratingly seemed to show a marked falling off of temperatures in the second half of the 20th century, which showed that they were not proxies for temperature at all. It was this problem that led to the most quoted of all the Climategate emails, describing how they had used 'Mike's *Nature* trick' to 'hide the decline'. In other words, they had cut off the tree-ring sequence just where it wasn't giving the picture they wanted, and then, like Mann, incorporated thermometer temperatures for recent decades, making them look much warmer than the medieval era.

Once out in the open, the 'hockey-stick' controversy continued tortuously to roll on for two more years. Two of Mann's closest academic colleagues, publicly championed by Houghton, pulled out all the stops to ensure that the next IPCC report, due in 2007, would include evidence confirming the accuracy of the 'hockey stick'.[35]

In fact, since 2001, there had been two significant changes at the top of the IPCC. Houghton himself had stepped down as head of Working Group I, responsible for the science of climate change. In 2002, it had been given, for political reasons, a new chairman, Dr Rajendra Pachauri, the obscure director of a small, Delhi-based research institute, TERI. Pachauri had formerly been a railway engineer, before getting a PhD in the 'economics of energy'. He had no background in climate science.[36]

In 2006 Mann's graph was the subject of two separate Congressional inquiries. One included several of his supporters, who made sure that its findings were not too obviously damaging. The other commissioned a report from Dr Edward Wegman, one of America's most respected statisticians, which was fiercely critical of Mann's methodology. In a line which could almost have come from Irving Janis, Wegman wrote that Mann's academic supporters were

> ...a tightly-knit group of individuals who passionately believe in their thesis. However, our perception is that this group has a self-reinforcing feedback mechanism.

In other words, the group's method was to discuss, peer-review and cite each other's work, to maximise the authority of their shared view. But despite all their efforts, carefully orchestrated by their allies inside the IPCC, and despite further breaches of the IPCC's strict prohibition on citing papers not yet published, the final report's defence of Mann was pretty well buried away. Its only repetition of his graph was so scrambled together with others in a 'spaghetti' diagram that it was barely visible.

Although the 'hockey stick' had now been so widely discredited that it had all but sunk from view, it would continue to be used by supporters of the 'consensus' as if none of this had happened. In the eyes of politicians and the media, the prestige of the IPCC remained as high as ever.

9 When groupthink meets the outside world

Sir David King goes to Moscow

> They revealed an absolute – and I stress absolute – inability to answer questions … when it became clear that they could not provide a substantive answer to a question … attempts were made to disrupt the seminar. At least four times during the course of the seminar, ugly scenes were staged which prevented the seminar from proceeding normally. As a result we lost at least four hours of working time.

Vladimir Putin's chief economic adviser speaking of the behaviour of the British delegation led by Sir David King at an international conference on global warming in Moscow in 2004

History can provide few more remarkable examples of the power of groupthink than the scale on which, by the early years of the 21st century, the supporters of the 'consensus' had now taken over every major scientific institution in the Western world.[37] Every prestigious scientific body, led by the Royal Society in Britain and the National Academy of Sciences in America, every reputable scientific journal such as *Nature* and *Science*, every university (and pretty well the entire education system) was by now not just committed to the official orthodoxy but evangelising for the cause.

Scientists from almost any discipline were vying to produce ever more scary scenarios of how polar ice would melt, sea levels rise, and droughts, floods, hurricanes and killer heatwaves become more frequent, not least because this was now the easiest way to get access to public funding for any research which could be related, however tangentially, to 'climate change'.

But these scientists and academics were all operating from within the 'consensus' bubble. This meant that they only talked to each other, confident that they all shared the same a-priori assumptions. In their exchanges with their colleagues and at their endless publicly-funded conferences, they never met anyone who might disagree with them or ask awkward questions.

But we now recall two examples of what happened on the very rare occasions when those inside the bubble inadvertently came up against genuine experts from outside it. The first was the experience of Sir David King who, since 2000, had been the chief scientific adviser to the British government under Tony Blair. In 2004, with the US still failing to ratify Kyoto, Blair was bidding to take the international lead in getting enough countries to ratify the treaty for it to come into force. And he now sent King into battle to support him.

As a specialist in surface chemistry, King had no qualifications in climate science whatever. But in January 2004 this did not stop him writing in *Science* that global warming was now the 'most severe' problem facing mankind, 'a far greater threat to the world than terrorism'. King attacked President George W. Bush for failing to bring the US, as the world's largest carbon dioxide emitter, into line (overlooking the fact that it was the US Senate that had unanimously vetoed even signing the treaty, let alone ratifying it).

In March, King went much further, warning a committee of MPs that the South Pole had already lost 40 percent of its ice and that the melting of the polar ice caps could cause a shift in the Gulf Stream, which would lower temperatures in Britain and Europe by as much as 10°C. This 'could happen quite suddenly', said King, as could the 'switching off' of the Indian monsoon. 'There could be a point, and it is quite likely', he went on, where temperatures rose too high for tropical forests to survive, 'so that they would switch from being net absorbers of carbon dioxide to net emitters'. This could trigger a repeat of what had happened 55 million years ago, when carbon dioxide rose to 1000 parts per million of the atmosphere. Most of the Earth was so hot that this made 'Antarctica virtually the only place on the planet which was habitable'.[38]

The British politicians might have been ready to believe all this, but four months later King found a very different audience when, at Blair's request, he led a team of British scientists to Moscow, to take part in an international seminar organised for the Russian Academy of Sciences by President Putin's chief economic adviser, Alexander Ilarionov. King's mission was to persuade the Russians to ratify Kyoto, which would at last bring the treaty into force. But Russia's leading scientists could not have been more opposed to the Western 'consensus' that carbon dioxide was the chief driver of global warming. And when King saw that the list of speakers invited to address the conference included some of the world's leading scientists who were most sceptical of the IPCC 'consensus', he furiously described them as 'undesirables', saying that they should not be allowed to speak.[39]

When it was insisted that the seminar would continue as planned, the gathering was astonished by the behaviour of King and his colleagues. They ran on for much longer than their allotted time, frequently interrupted other speakers, and on four occasions caused the proceedings to break up in such disorder that they had to be suspended. The climax came when King himself was at the podium, putting forward the 'consensus' view on one of its favourite memes: that global warming was responsible for the melting of the ice cap on Kilimanjaro. One of those in the audience who could see that King had no idea what he was talking about was Professor Paul Reiter, the world's leading authority on insect-borne diseases, such as malaria. As an adviser to the World Health Organization, he had contributed to the IPCC's 1996 report, but had been strongly critical of its claim that global warming would cause a spread of diseases. And he had already aroused King's ire at the conference, by detailing where the IPCC had got the science on his own subject so badly wrong.

Reiter now stood up to explain politely that King seemed unaware of the several expert studies which had shown that the shrinking of the Kilimanjaro ice cap had nothing to do with global warming. The ice had been melting since the 1880s. Most of its retreat had been in the years before 1950. Its cause had been local deforestation, which had led to a severe drop in precipitation. Unable to answer Reiter's points, King broke off mid-sentence of a halting reply and led his team out of the room.

At the end of proceedings, Ilarionov called a press conference to speak angrily about all they had witnessed. He began by recalling that months earlier the Russian Academy had sent nine questions on science to the IPCC, to which they had been offered nothing in reply but political exhortations for Russia to ratify the treaty. Nothing in the Kyoto Protocol itself, he said, or 'the "scientific" theory on which it is based' had been 'borne out by the data'. The predicted consequences of global warming, 'increased droughts, floods, hurricanes or other extreme weather events' had simply not taken place. If there was:

> ...an insignificant increase in the temperature, it is not due to anthropogenic factors but to natural factors connected with planet itself and solar activity.

He went on to speak witheringly about the 'distorted and falsified' data used to promote the 'consensus', mentioning the 'hockey stick'. And he then tore apart the behaviour of King and his colleagues, pointing out their complete inability to answer scientific questions and referring to those 'ugly scenes' that had 'prevented the seminar from proceeding normally'.

Ilarionov ended with a peroration warning that the world seemed, once again, to be up against a 'man-hating, totalitarian ideology', dealing in 'misinformation, falsification, fabrication, mythology and propaganda', in an attempt 'to prove the alleged validity' of its theory. No one listening to this storming rejection of all the 'consensus' stood for could have guessed that, four months later, on a private initiative by Tony Blair, President Putin would do a complete U-turn. In return for Russia being allowed to join the World Trade Organization on very favourable terms, it would now ratify the Kyoto Treaty.

An insider's account of the IPCC

> The issue of consensus is key to understanding the limitations of IPCC pronouncements. Consensus is the stuff of politics, not of science...in the age of information, popular knowledge of scientific information...is awash in the tide of misinformation... Alarmist activists operating in well-funded advocacy groups have a lead role in creating this misinformation. In many cases they manipulate public perceptions with emotive and fiercely judgmental 'scientific' pronouncements...Scientists who challenge these alarmists are rarely given priority by the media...
>
> Professor Paul Reiter, evidence to House of Lords committee, 2005

The following year, in 2005, came another of the rare occasions when leading spokesmen for the 'consensus' were brought together with some of the world's most prominent scientific 'sceptics', this time in London, as witnesses called before the House of Lords Select Committee on Economic Affairs.

On one side, among others, were Dr Rajendra Pachauri, the chairman of the IPCC, Sir John Houghton and Sir David King. Witnesses for the other side, at the insistence of a minority of the committee, such as the sceptical Lord (Nigel) Lawson, included Dr Richard Lindzen, Professor Ross McKitrick, Professor Niklaus Morner, a former president of the International Commission on Sea Level Change (another highly sceptical former contributor to the IPCC whose evidence had irked King in Moscow) and Professor Reiter.

The two sides did not, of course, meet face to face, but gave evidence individually. The representatives of the 'consensus', expounding the standard IPCC line and praising the value of its computer models, were clearly not pleased to see that prominent sceptics would also be giving evidence. They went out of their way to disparage what Houghton described as representatives of only the 'very few' scientists who disagreed with the IPCC. They were, he said, 'not seriously regarded'.

But the most revealing session was that featuring Professor Reiter, because, having been a contributing author to the chapter of its 1996 report dealing with the effects of global warming on human health, he was able to give a unique insider's view of how the IPCC actually worked.

Reiter recalled how startled he had been to discover that almost none of his fellow contributors to the chapter were in any way qualified experts on its subject. One had written a paper on health and cell phones, although his main interest was the 'effectiveness of motor-cycle helmets'. None of the chapter's lead authors had written a research paper on insect-borne diseases and two of them were full-time 'environmental activists', one having written articles on land mines and mercury poisoning. Their sole purpose, it emerged, was to produce a chapter showing how warming would produce a spreading of 'vector-borne diseases', as 'predicted' by an absurdly simplistic computer model.

In vain had Reiter tried to explain that all serious science showed that there was no evidence to support this view. But, sure enough, when he saw the finished chapter, he was appalled to see how its 'amateurish text' was riddled with basic scientific errors, reflecting only 'the limited knowledge' of its authors.

The IPCC had got what it was after. The Summary for Policymakers was able to claim that 'climate change is likely to have wide-ranging and mostly adverse effects on human health, with significant loss of life'. After the report had been widely acclaimed as representing 'the consensus of the world's 1500 top scientists', Reiter noted how 'eight out of nine major websites' had put insect-borne diseases 'at the top of the list of adverse impacts of climate change, quoting the IPCC'. He described how he had then been invited back to contribute to the IPCC's 2001 report, but when he had found that he and one other author were the only scientists with any knowledge of insect-borne diseases at all, and that the other authors only wanted the same alarmist story as before, he resigned.

For the 2007 report, as the world's leading authority on the subject, he had actually been nominated to be a lead author by the US government. But this time he was rejected. When he asked an IPCC official why, it turned out that she worked for the UK Met Office's Hadley Centre. She could only tell him that the selection of authors was decided by 'the governments of the world'. As Reiter told the House of Lords committee, having comprehensively demonstrated the point, 'consensus is the stuff of politics, not of science'.

10 The 'consensus' and the media

The BBC decides to break the law for the 'consensus'

> The BBC must do all it can to ensure that controversial subjects are treated with due accuracy and impartiality in all its relevant output.
>
> Statutory obligation under the BBC Charter, 2006

> I found the seminar frankly shocking…I was frankly appalled at the level of ignorance of the issue which the BBC people showed. It seemed to me that none of them had shown even a modicum of professional curiosity on the subject…I spent the day discussing the subject and I don't recall anyone showing any sign of having read anything serious at all'.
>
> Richard D. North, after attending BBC seminar on 'Climate Change: The Challenge to Broadcasting', 26 January 2006[40]

Just as the entire scientific establishment was firmly in the grip of the 'consensus', so were the Western media. In the US, every leading newspaper and journal, from the *New York Times* and the *Washington Post* to *Time* and *Newsweek*, had become its fully committed supporters, as had all its major television channels, NBC, CBS and ABC.

In Britain the picture was the same. Newspapers such as the *Guardian*, the *Independent* and the *Observer* were such fervent evangelists for the cause that the only way they differed from the IPCC orthodoxy lay in the zest with which they wanted to push it even further, by eagerly printing every new global warming scare story that came their way.

Often these originated from the main environmental campaigning groups, such as Greenpeace, Friends of the Earth and WWF, which had become the 'armed wing' of the global warming movement, constantly claiming that catastrophic climate change was now advancing faster than even the IPCC had predicted, and urging governments to take much more drastic action.

Scarcely a single British journalist ever questioned this hysteria. But one exception was Rosemary Righter, the chief leader writer of the *Times*, who described to the House of Lords committee a very peculiar conference of 200 scientists that had taken place at Exeter University early in 2005. It had been staged at the behest of Tony Blair, shortly due to host a meeting of the G8 governments, who planned to put global warming at the top of its agenda. The gathering, she said,

> ...became something like a contest between which horror stories – the Vanishing Gulf Stream, Millions Dead of Malaria in the Midlands, the Parboiled Polar Bear – would do the best job of making the public's flesh creep. As spin for the government's case that climate change is a threat greater than terrorism, this was no doubt effective. As guidance to policy-makers, it was a disgrace. Tall stories have no place at G8 summits.[41]

In fact, far and away the most prominent publicist for such 'consensus-plus' alarmism in the British media was the BBC, which had reported that conference in glowing terms. And in January 2006, it went still further by staging behind closed doors a very peculiar event of its own at its White City Television Centre.

What was later to become notorious as 'the BBC's secret seminar' lasted a whole day, and featured 28 of the BBC's most senior executives, including the heads of television and radio news, current affairs and 'Vision'. They were all meeting to discuss 'Climate Change: The Challenge to Broadcasting', along with twenty-eight of what the BBC Trust was to refer to in its 2007 report as 'some of the best scientific experts' on the subject.

The event's resident organiser was one of the BBC's chief environmental correspondents, Roger Harrabin, who had long been familiar for his relentlessly one-sided reports on climate change. Harrabin also ran a small outfit dedicated to changing the way environmental stories were covered in the broadcast media, called the Cambridge Media and Environment Programme, with funding from the WWF, the Department for the Environment, Food and Rural Affairs and the University of East Anglia. It was through this body that Harrabin organised the seminar.

For a long time, the BBC tried to keep secret what had gone on at this meeting, or who these 'best scientific experts' had actually been: apart from the fact that its keynote speaker was Lord May of Oxford. Best known as an ecologist, he had formerly been a trustee of the WWF and President of the Royal Society, which under his aegis between 2000 and 2005 had been transformed into another body relentlessly evangelising for the warming cause.

May's views were typified by his valedictory address to the Royal Society, when he said:

> ...there exists a climate-change 'denial' lobby, funded to the tune of tens of millions of dollars by sections of the hydrocarbon industry, which was very similar in attitude and tactics to the tobacco lobby that continues to deny smoking causes cancer, or the curious lobby that denies HIV causes AIDS.

Only one dissenter had inadvertently been invited to the seminar: journalist Richard D. North described, in the words quoted above, how 'appalled' he had been at the complete 'ignorance' on the subject of everyone from the BBC to whom he had spoken.

Only five years later did a search of the Wayback Machine, an archive of internet web pages, finally reveal who those 'best scientific experts' in fact had been. Only three were active scientists at all, none of them climate experts (and one was head of the university department at East Anglia which helped fund Harrabin's propaganda outfit). Virtually all the rest were professional climate lobbyists, ranging from emissaries of Greenpeace and the Stop Climate Chaos campaign to the 'carbon dioxide project manager' for the BP oil company (which two years earlier had advertised that its initials no longer stood for 'British Petroleum' but 'Beyond Petroleum', in an effort to show that it was now as dubious about fossil fuels as any oil company could pretend to be).

But the real significance of this meeting was that, on the advice of Lord May, the BBC decided that it no longer need be troubled by its statutory duty under the BBC Charter to report on 'controversial subjects' only with 'due accuracy and impartiality'. From now on it would argue that the scientific consensus in favour of man-made climate change was so overwhelming that there simply were no longer two sides to the argument at all. What Lord May called 'the climate-change denial lobby' was now so insignificant and discredited that it would be perfectly 'accurate' and 'impartial' to ignore it altogether (although, to be fair, there had been little sign that this was not the BBC's policy already).

Four months later the BBC celebrated its new 'freedom' by launching what it called its 'Climate Chaos' season: a whole series of programmes launched with a two-part documentary starring the most revered of all its presenters, Sir David Attenborough, entitled *The Truth About Climate Change*. Attenborough introduced himself as someone who had once been sceptical about man-made climate change, but now realised that the evidence for it was 'overwhelming'. What had changed his mind were the 'climatologists'' graphs showing such a close correlation between rising carbon dioxide levels and rising temperatures. He then ran through some examples of the terrifying damage already being caused by global warming. Only the previous year there had been the catastrophic devastation caused by Hurricane Katrina, which a warming world would now be likely to see much more of. There had also been a drought in the Amazon so severe that it threatened the survival of the world's largest rainforest. The freak European heatwave in 2003, the 'worst for 60 years', had killed '27,000 people', and such events were predicted to become much more frequent. Ice in the Arctic was disappearing so fast that it threatened the survival of polar bears. And it was said that the speed at which Greenland's ice cap was melting threatened such a catastrophic rise in sea levels that, in his second programme, Attenborough was to claim that this would flood much of southern Britain and wipe most of Florida and all of Bangladesh off the map.

All these claims were familiar from climate activists. But had Attenborough consulted any proper science he would have known that every one of them was a complete travesty of the facts. Far from becoming more frequent, there were now fewer Atlantic hurricanes than in the 1940s. The flooding of New Orleans was not due to global warming but the failure to maintain the levees that protected low-lying parts of the city from the lake and river above them. Attenborough omitted to mention that the 2005 Amazon drought had already been succeeded in

2006 by record rains and flooding across the Amazon basin.

Meteorologists had explained that the 2003 heatwave had not been due to global warming but to hot air sucked up from the Sahara by a prolonged high-pressure cell over western Europe. And those '27,000' deaths were much fewer than the numbers commonly ascribed to excessive cold in European winters.

Studies had shown that summer temperatures in the Arctic were even higher at the end of the warming period between 1920 and 1940 than they had become since. It was estimated that, since the 1960s, polar bear numbers in parts of the Arctic Circle had quadrupled. As for the melting of Greenland's ice cap, Attenborough could have discovered that this amounted to only seven one-thousandths of one percent of its total volume, which evidence showed must have shrunk significantly more during the Medieval Warm Period, when there were human settlements now buried under feet of ice. As for those sea levels, they were currently rising by only 2 millimetres a year and even the IPCC was predicting that, over the next century, they would rise no more than 59 centimetres (23 inches).

The real point is that it never crossed the minds of Attenborough and the BBC to do the research which could have shown them just how seriously adrift from the facts they were. So hermetically sealed were they in their bubble that they wouldn't even have known where to look.

Altogether the BBC provided a perfect example of Janis's three rules of groupthink. First, they had become caught up in a 'narrative' that bore no relation to external reality. Second, by talking only to those who agreed with the narrative, they convinced themselves that this was the 'consensus' view with which all right-thinking people agreed. Third, they then agreed, as was illustrated by their seminar, that those who disagreed were so wrong-headed and few in number that they could legally be ignored.

Later that year an even more striking example was to follow.

11 Hysteria reaches its height

The inconvenient untruths of Mr Gore

> A secret report, suppressed by US defence chiefs and obtained by The *Observer*, warns that major European cities will be sunk beneath rising seas as Britain is plunged into a 'Siberian' climate by 2020. Nuclear conflict, mega-droughts, famine and widespread rioting will spread across the world...deaths from war and famine run into the millions, until the planet's population is reduced by such an extent the Earth can cope. Access to water becomes a major battleground...Rich areas like the US and Europe would become 'virtual fortresses', to prevent millions of migrants from entering, after being forced from land drowned by sea-level rise or no longer able to grow crops.
>
> *The Observer*, 11 November 2004[42]

> It is irresponsible, reckless and deeply amoral to question the seriousness of the situation. The time for diagnosis is over. The time to act is now.
>
> Gro Harlem Brundtland, 9 May 2007

> Almost everywhere, climate denial now looks as stupid and unacceptable as Holocaust denial.
>
> George Monbiot, *The Guardian*, 21 September 2006

If one event more than any marked the moment when the global warming hysteria reached its height, it was the launch in the summer of 2006 of the film designed to spread the message to a worldwide mass-audience: Al Gore's *An Inconvenient Truth*.

Cinemas were soon packed out to watch the highest-earning documentary in Hollywood history, breathlessly acclaimed by the BBC's Richard Black as 'perhaps the most terrifying movie of all time'. It was not only to win an Oscar but, for Gore, an equal share with the IPCC in that year's Nobel Peace Prize.

Opening with shots of melting glaciers and those vanishing snows of Kilimanjaro, Gore's method was to round up every familiar global warming scare story so far devised and then to exaggerate it still further.

His *pièce de résistance*, supposed to confirm the accuracy of the 'hockey stick' (so cruelly traduced by 'global warming sceptics' who were now 'diminishing as fast as those mountain glaciers'), was to stand in front of a huge and even more terrifying version of his own, which he claimed was based on ice cores taken from glaciers by his 'friend' Dr Lonnie Thompson. This culminated in an upward tick so much more dramatic than anything previously seen that Gore had to be hoisted up on a lift to reach it.

From there on audiences were treated to a graphic sequence of horror stores: polar bears drowning as the Arctic ice melted, computer graphics showing how many of the world's most famous cities would disappear as sea levels rose by 20 feet, and the world's climate system thrown into chaos by floods, droughts, tornadoes and hurricanes like nothing ever seen before.

Little islands in the Pacific, like Tuvalu, would soon be vanishing beneath the waves. The melting of the Himalayan glaciers, on which seven major river systems depended, would eventually rob 40 percent of the world's population of water. Global warming would lead to a mass-extinction of species, which were already disappearing at a rate '1000 percent' faster than before. There would be an explosion in the incidence of malaria and other 'vector-borne' diseases, as rising temperatures allowed insects to spread from the tropics over the globe.

This apocalyptic vision, Gore claimed, was now endorsed by 'every climate scientist in the world' (apart of course from that tiny handful of sceptics who were 'diminishing as fast as those mountain glaciers'). And in support of this he cited a recent study by Naomi Oreskes, a lecturer in 'the history of science' and passionate believer in the 'consensus' on climate change. According to Gore, she had analysed 928 'peer-reviewed' scientific papers dealing with climate change and found that the percentage expressing any doubts about the cause of global warming was exactly 'zero'.

Scarcely a single statement in Gore's film stood up to examination as being even remotely true. Some such points have already been referred to: the shrinking of the ice sheets on Kilimanjaro and Greenland; the science fiction projections of likely future rises in sea-levels; the alleged increase in Atlantic hurricanes; the claim that warming would bring a massive spread in insect-borne diseases.

One of the most laughable, however, was the blow-up temperature graph which supposedly confirmed the accuracy of Mann's 'hockey stick', and which Gore claimed was based on Dr Thompson's glacier ice-cores. For a start, a search of Thompson's work showed that his studies had only been concerned with measuring past precipitation, not temperatures. But still more damningly, it turned out that the only real source for Gore's graph was a slightly amended and exaggerated version of Mann's 'hockey stick' itself. The only evidence Gore could produce to prove that Mann's graph was accurate was a version of the very graph he was defending.

Claim after claim, when measured against the scientific literature, simply fell apart: from his alleged increases in floods, droughts and tornadoes to his claims about the causes and rate of species extinctions. If the Himalayan glaciers were receding, this was because of a pall of ash clouds from forests being burned in Indonesia to make way for palm-oil plantations. Satellite observations showed that sea levels around Tuvalu and other supposedly threatened Pacific islands, far from rising, had actually been falling.

On nothing was Gore more embarrassingly caught out than his sequence showing polar bears supposedly drowning because global warming had melted the ice. This was inspired by a picture taken in 2005 of four bears drowned, not by lack of ice, but by an unusually severe storm off the coast of Alaska.

As for his use of Oreskes' paper on 'The scientific consensus on climate change' to claim that not one of her 928 papers had expressed doubt about the causes of global warming, her study had in fact made clear that she based this only on the 'abstracts' of her sample. It was this which led her to claim that 75 percent of them endorsed the 'consensus' that global warming was man-made. But subsequent analysis of the papers found that only 905 had included abstracts, and of these only 13, or 2 percent, explicitly endorsed anthropogenic climate change. The vast majority did not mention it at all.[43]

A superficial observer of the unbridgeable gulf between Gore's film and scientific fact might have been tempted to describe it as an exercise in 'fraud'. But this would be to imply that Gore had known very well what he was doing and deliberately set out to deceive the public. Psychologically, however, this would be a crucial misunderstanding of how groupthink works. In making most of their film's errors, Gore and his production team would simply not have been aware of all the scientific studies showing that their facts were wrong. They were not concerned with facts. Their sole preoccupation had been with assembling a 'narrative', which they wished to be as persuasive and powerful as they could make it.

The point is that, by definition, groupthink is never grounded in reality; it is a belief-system. And the purpose of those caught up in it, and who are so convinced of the moral rightness of their cause, is to convert others to share their beliefs. It is not the real facts which matter; it is the pseudo-facts that can be used to make their narrative seem most compelling.

It is in this way that, for any form of groupthink, the ends come to justify the means. The most interesting chapter in Hitler's *Mein Kampf* is that on 'Propaganda', because it so well reflected the way in which the supreme purpose of any such belief-system is to find the most effective way of uniting all those who already share it into a seemingly irresistible 'consensus', and thus to win over others to their cause. This is why groupthink always sees as its real enemies those who refuse to go along with it, and who try to point out that the Emperor is not wearing any clothes.

Gore himself had earlier in the year compared scientists sceptical of the 'consensus' with 'members of the "Flat Earth Society"' or with 'the people who believe the moon landing was actually staged in a movie lot in Arizona'. But in the excitement following the success of his film, the *Guardian* journalist George Monbiot picked up from America a new and even more damning term for such people. To deny man-made climate change, he wrote, now 'looks as stupid and unacceptable as Holocaust denial'.

Others had been branding 'climate sceptics' as 'deniers' as long ago as 2002. Lord May had spoken of 'the climate-change denial lobby' to those BBC executives at their 'secret seminar' in 2006. But equating them with the little bunch of neo-Nazi cranks who deny the reality of Hitler's death camps gave the term a wholly new, morally-charged edge. From now on, to dismiss them all as just 'deniers' caught on like wildfire, precisely because it carried this new and venomous sub-text.

It was perhaps no coincidence that, two days before Monbiot's article was published, an American 'green' blog had given extravagant praise to his latest book. It ended with this battle-cry:

> When we've finally gotten serious about global warming, when the impacts are really hitting us, and we're in a full worldwide scramble to minimise the damage, we should have war-crimes trials for these bastards, some sort of climate Nuremberg.[44]

One reason why supporters of the 'consensus' were finding new and more extreme language to express their hostility was that the 'deniers' were now finding new and more disconcerting ways in which to challenge them.

12 The story begins to change: dissenting voices

> 2007 is likely to be the warmest year on record.
>
> UK Met Office press release, 4 February 2007

> It is another nail in the coffin of the climate change deniers and represents the most authoritative picture to date, showing that the debate over the science of climate change is well and truly over.
>
> David Miliband, UK Environment Secretary, at launch of the IPCC's Fourth Assessment Report, 2 February 2007

The Great Global Warming Swindle

At the start of 2007, it might have seemed that the 'consensus' was sweeping all before it more than ever. On 2 February, to unprecedented hype, the IPCC launched in Paris the Summary for Policymakers for its Fourth Assessment Report. In every respect this lavishly-produced document, co-written at the headquarters of his TERI institute in Delhi by the IPCC's chairman Dr Pachauri, went much further than any of its predecessors. 'Warming of the climate system', it pronounced, was now 'unequivocal'. Temperatures in the Northern Hemisphere were now 'the highest in at least 1300 years'. Polar ice and snow cover were in sharp decline. Sea levels were dangerously rising. Hurricanes, heatwaves, floods and droughts were all becoming more frequent. The Himalayan glaciers could be all-but gone by 2035. Droughts were threatening to destroy nearly half the Amazon rainforest, and by 2050 could have halved crop yields across Africa.

Hours later, BBC television news led its early evening news with pictures of power station cooling towers belching out 'pollution' (i.e. steam), cars submerged in floodwater and a mass of ice calving from an Antarctic glacier, all stamped in red with the word GUILTY. In a doom-laden but triumphant voice, the newsreader announced:

> At 6 o'clock – there's no doubt. Climate change is happening – and we are to blame. Leading scientists predict that by the end of the century, some parts of the world will be too hot to live in. As temperatures soar and sea levels rise, the verdict from the world's leading climate scientists: the human race is guilty of global warming.

Among the world's politicians who had been on hand to give the media all the soundbites they wanted was France's President Jacques Chirac, claiming that the world was now faced with such an 'emergency' that it was 'at the doorstep of the irreversible'. 'Half-measures' were no longer enough. Another was the UK's David Miliband, acclaiming the report as the 'final nail in the coffin of the climate change deniers'. On returning home he arranged for DVDs of Al Gore's film to be sent for showing in every secondary school in Britain.[45]

In March 2007, at a meeting of the European Council, the heads of the EU's 27 governments unanimously agreed that they would act to stop global temperatures from rising by more than 2°C, introducing a package of measures to show that the EU was now 'leading the world in the fight against climate change'. By 2020, it would have reduced its emissions of carbon dioxide by 20 percent. No less than 20 percent of all the EU's energy would by then come from 'renewables', such as wind, solar and 'biomass'. Ten percent of all transport fuel would be powered, not by fossil fuels, but by 'biofuels' made from crops such as wheat, maize, sugar beet and palm oil. And by 2010 the sale of conventional incandescent light bulbs would be banned, to be replaced with low-energy 'compact fluorescent lamps'. Ironically, these contained significant quantities of mercury, which five years earlier the EU had banned as a 'hazardous substance'.

A few weeks earlier, however, millions of British viewers had been treated to another film like nothing seen on television before. *The Great Global Warming Swindle*, 90 minutes long, brought together for the first time a whole array of leading 'sceptical' scientists to explain why they could not accept the 'consensus' view. These included Richard Lindzen, Fred Singer, Paul Reiter and Dr Syun-ichi Akasofu, the former head of the International Arctic Research Center in Alaska. Dr Roy Spencer and Dr John Christy had come to their sceptical view as the scientists in charge of one of the official global temperature records measured by satellites, at the University of Alabama.[46] Other experts featured in the programme included Dr Nir Shaviv from Israel and Dr Eigel Friis-Christensen from Denmark (a colleague of Dr Henrik Svensmark[47]), whose work had separately confirmed how crucially influential on the Earth's temperatures and climate were fluctuations in the activity of the Sun; Dr Pat Michaels, a senior US meteorologist and longtime prominent sceptic; Dr Karl Wunsch, a leading US oceanographer; Dr Ian Clark, an expert on ice-cores; Paul Driesser, who had written a book on how measures to combat climate change were damaging the lives of millions of people in the Third World by holding them back from the use of fossil fuels which might help to lift them out of poverty; and Patrick Moore, a co-founder of Greenpeace, describing why the scientific evidence had led him to change his mind.[48]

So authoritatively did all these and other experts explain, from different angles, why they believed that the IPCC had got it seriously wrong in assuming that rising carbon dioxide was the chief cause of recent warming that the programme met with a howl of outrage from advocates of the 'consensus'. George Monbiot in the *Guardian* savaged its contributors as 'cranks' talking 'bunkum', whose views had long been 'discredited' by proper scientists. Hundreds of official complaints poured in to the broadcasting regulator Ofcom, including one collection signed by '37 professors' (including Phil Jones of the CRU); another of 175 pages, supported by, among others, Bert Bolin; and one from the IPCC itself, supported by Dr Pachauri and Sir John Houghton.

So vast was the mountain of complaints that it was to take Ofcom a year to process them. But so strongly was Channel 4 able to support all it had said that the vast majority were rejected. Ofcom avoided the main issue by claiming that, since the science on global warming was generally accepted, the programme could not have misled its viewers, as alleged. By way of modest concession, it did criticise Channel 4 on four minor procedural points (e.g. not allowing enough time for the IPCC to respond to questions). It also ruled that what Dr Wunsch said on camera in his interview had been shown 'out of context', and that Sir David King had been misrepresented as having said precisely what he did convey to those MPs about Antarctica becoming the only habitable place on the planet.

No sooner was the Ofcom report published than press statements were issued from Pachauri, saying he was 'pleased' that Ofcom had 'upheld most of the complaints' and the IPCC's 'credibility' (wholly untrue); and Houghton, saying how pleased he was that Ofcom has 'recognised' the film's 'serious inaccuracies' (it had done nothing of the kind). But this did not stop the BBC headlining its report on the ruling: 'Climate documentary "broke rules"'.

In media eyes, the champions of the 'consensus' had spun victory out of a defeat. But they were now becoming uncomfortably aware of a rather more serious threat to their previously unchallenged ability to dominate the public 'debate'.

The rise of the 'counter-consensus'

> Global warming has become a symbol and example of the clash between truth and propaganda. The one politically correct truth has already been established, and opposing it is not easy. Yet a large number of people, including top scientists, see the issue of climate change, its causes and its proposed consequences quite differently.
>
> Vaclav Klaus, President of the Czech Republic, *Blue Planet in Green Shackles*

Until the early years of the 21st century, the 'consensus' had enjoyed no more useful an ally than the mainstream media. On both sides of the Atlantic, every leading newspaper and television channel had long been so actively committed to the cause that the 'consensus' exercised an almost total monopoly on information generally available to the public. Something was now happening, however, which was dramatically changing the nature of the debate. This was the arrival of the internet. The nature of the discussion was now being opened up in a way which a few years earlier would have seemed unimaginable. This had effect in at least two obvious ways. One was simply the colossal increase in the availability of information. At the click of a button it was now possible to have instant access to tens of thousands of scientific papers, IPCC and other official reports, data on anything from global temperatures to changes in the extent of polar ice or the percentage of electricity being generated by windmills: every kind of information which might formerly have taken days or even months to obtain.

The other way in which the internet was beginning to add a whole new dimension to the debate was the rise of a number of expert specialist blogs. These were allowing informed technical discussions to take place with an intensity of interchange which not even scientific journals could emulate. It was here, for instance, that in 2003 Steve McIntyre had, on his website, first begun revealing his discovery of the startling technical flaws in the 'hockey stick'. This so irked Michael Mann and his colleagues that, the following year, with the aid of a PR firm that specialised in representing 'liberal' causes, they launched a blog of their own, *RealClimate*, to counter McIntyre's charges. Calling themselves the 'Hockey Team' – they included Gavin Schmidt and Phil Jones, the men in charge of the official global surface temperature records – they liked to claim that they were the 'real' climate scientists, while McIntyre and McKitrick should be ignored as just unqualified 'amateurs'. This in turn prompted McIntyre to counter-attack by launching his own regular blog, *Climate Audit*. The trouble was that, in his own field of expertise, statistics, McIntyre was able to run rings round them, as he continued to dissect each new trick these members of the IPCC establishment tried to play.

In 2007 McIntyre teamed up with another new blog, *Watts Up With That?*, run by a Californian meteorologist, Anthony Watts. Watts' particular concern at this time was to check out every one of the thousands of weather stations across the US which provided temperature data to the US and Global Historical Climatology Networks (GHCN). The vast majority of these stations, this research revealed, did not begin to meet the official requirements for reliability, because they were situated on heat-absorbing asphalt, near airport runways, heated buildings or heat-emitting machinery such as air-conditioning units. Their measurements were thus being significantly distorted. Yet these same weather stations contributed a quite disproportionate share of the data used to compile the two global surface temperature records, GISS and HadCRUt, on which the IPCC and governments relied for their picture of how much the world was warming.

These findings led McIntyre to investigate the temperature records maintained for the US Historical Climate Network by Hansen and Schmidt at GISS. Here he made the startling discovery that these had been systematically 'adjusted', to make older temperatures look cooler and more recent temperatures higher than those actually recorded. The GISS website, for instance, now showed that 1998 was the hottest year in the US record, and that five of the hottest years ever recorded had been since 1990. But the originally measured data had shown that 1934 was significantly warmer than 1998, and that four of the hottest years in the record were in those same 'dustbowl' years of the 1930s.

McIntyre then moved on to look at what GISS had been doing with temperatures in the Arctic. A paper published by Hansen in 1987 had shown that temperatures there too had been higher in the 1930s than at any time since.[49] But again these had now been given the same two-way 'adjustment', to show recent years as having been comparatively much warmer than the originally recorded data justified.

To track this down did not need any knowledge of 'climate science'. As with the 'hockey stick', it simply required the expertise to uncover what key supporters of the 'consensus' were doing with the electronic evidence. In groupthink terms, this yet again confirmed just how dubious the methods being used to support their theory were too often turning out to be. What was more generally happening at this time, with the aid of the internet, was that experts from outside the 'consensus' were combining their information to form a kind of informal 'counter-consensus' to the orthodoxy that had ruled the roost ever since the great alarm over global warming had been launched on its way in 1988.

At the end of 2007 a minority report from the US Senate Environment Committee was able to list and quote more than 400 scientists from 20 countries around the world, many past or current contributors to the IPCC, who were now prepared to express their dissent from the 'consensus', sometimes in the strongest terms. They included Nobel prizewinners and academics from many of the world's leading universities, such as Harvard, MIT, Princeton and London, in disciplines ranging from climatology, oceanography and physics, to biology, geology and chemistry. They even included members of the National Academy of Sciences and employees of NASA and the National Oceanographic and Atmospheric Administration (NOAA).

Several admitted that, having previously been supporters of the 'consensus', the evidence had now led them to change their minds. Many testified to the pressure they and like-minded colleagues had been under not to make their dissenting views known. Not the least distinguished of them was Dr Syun-icho Akasofu, formerly director of the International Arctic Research Center, who wrote that 'the method of study adopted by the IPCC is fundamentally flawed, resulting in a baseless conclusion'.

In early 2008, an unprecedented conference was staged in New York by the Heartland Institute, a US free-market think-tank, bringing together hundreds of scientists from a wide range of disciplines, along with policy makers such as the President of the Czech Republic (quoted above). It was accompanied by a massive report, edited by Dr Fred Singer and compiled by 30 international scientists making up the 'Non-governmental Panel on Climate Change'.

Particularly under fire in this report and throughout the conference was the signal failure of the predictions made by IPCC computer models to be borne out by what were now 18 years of real-world evidence. One particular example analysed was the headline claim in the IPCC's 1996 report that the most telltale 'fingerprint' of global warming would be a rise in the temperature of the upper levels of the tropical troposphere. Satellite measurements had since consistently shown that no such 'fingerprint' existed. Virtually all the rise in temperatures had been seen, not in the troposphere, but near the earth's surface. This had been confirmed as early as 2000 by the National Academy of Sciences. Yet two subsequent IPCC reports had ignored this evidence that one of the more important predictions of its computer models was wrong.

At the end of the conference, those present endorsed a 'Manhattan Declaration' that, as the presence of so many reputable scientists had demonstrated, the claimed scientific 'consensus' on the extent and causes of global warming did not exist. They agreed that no convincing evidence had been produced to show that the climate was being influenced by man-made carbon dioxide rather than natural factors such as solar radiation and shifts in ocean currents, and that the hugely costly measures being adopted by governments in response to an imaginary problem would have no effect on the climate. The declaration ended by calling on world leaders to reject the position on climate change represented by the IPCC.[50]

For the British media, despite the standing of the more eminent scientists present, it was as if this conference had never taken place. But equally they seemed wholly oblivious to something of worldwide significance which was happening right under their noses.

All the five official records were showing that global temperatures had, between 2007 and 2008, dropped by around 0.7°C. This was equivalent to the entire net rise in world temperatures recorded through the whole of the 20th century. Even when, later in 2008, the temperature rose again, it became obvious that this did not alter the overall trend for the previous nine years. The records all still agreed that 1998 had been the hottest year in recent times, but that temperatures had then fallen; and since then, despite yearly fluctuations, the trend line had not risen at all. Two things about this were particularly significant.

The first was that 1998 had coincided with an unusually strong El Niño, and this had been followed by a La Niña, bringing a sharp drop in 2000. In 2006 there had been another rise, again coinciding with a strong El Niño, followed in 2007–8 by another strong La Niña and that marked drop in temperatures. Thus it seemed that by far the most obvious influence on the climate during the previous ten years had been nothing to do with carbon dioxide at all. It had been those fluctuating shifts in the world's ocean currents; in other words, a factor that was entirely natural.

Just as significant, therefore, was that none of this had been allowed for by those IPCC computer models on which the whole alarm over global warming ultimately rested. They had projected that, as carbon dioxide continued to rise, so warming would increase through the 21st century, by an average of 0.3°C per decade. So far nothing of the kind was happening.

As ever more people were coming to realise, climate models were looking in the wrong place for the causes of climate change.

13 Groupthink and wishful thinking

Britain's Climate Change Act, 2008

> As soon as a new dogma is implanted in the mind of crowds it becomes the source of inspiration...The sway it exerts over men's minds under these circumstances is absolute. Men of action have no thought beyond realising the accepted belief, legislators beyond applying it'.
>
> Gustave Le Bon, *The Crowd*

> It does not explain the unilateral and monstrous act of self-harm – or rather, the act of harm inflicted upon industrial Britain by Parliament – that was the Climate Change Act.
>
> Nick Timothy, *Conservative Home*, 5 April 2016

There is no more important key to understanding the nature of groupthink than to recognise the extent to which, because it is not rooted in reality, it is invariably based on some form of make-believe or wishful thinking. Those caught up in groupthink always have a view of the world, not as it really is, but as they imagine or would like it to be. That is why they only prefer to mix with others who share their view and remain so selective in the evidence they choose to accept. And it is because they cannot defend their beliefs against verifiable facts that they need to be so ruthlessly dismissive of anyone who produces evidence that seems to contradict them.

A good example of this in September 2008 was the BBC's response to Channel 4's *The Great Global Warming Swindle*: a three-part documentary series called *Earth: The Climate Wars*. Presented by a geologist as an 'objective' look at the whole global warming issue, the first and third programmes were standard restatements of the 'consensus' orthodoxy. But the real purpose of the series lay in its second programme, which set out to discredit some of the scientists who had taken part in Channel 4's documentary, including Dr Fred Singer and Dr Roy Spencer. This it did, first, by showing brief clips of interviews they had given at the Heartland conference. These were each carefully edited to make the scientists out of context look ridiculous, by showing them make some seemingly provocative point but without showing that in each case they had immediately continued with an explanation of how the point was scientifically justified.

The highpoint, however, was a wholly propagandist account of the 'hockey stick', complete with film of the presenter hugging one of Mann's famous bristlecone pines. This culminated in a bizarre sequence showing a huge poster of Mann's graph plastered over the side of an advertising truck, being wheeled triumphantly past Buckingham Palace, the Tower of London, Piccadilly Circus and all the major tourist spots of London.

At no point did the presenter give his baffled viewers any hint of what critics might have said to make this graph so controversial, and this was noted by many of the hundreds of letters sent to the BBC complaining about the programme's bias. Every one of these complaints, of course, was rejected. But what made this noteworthy was the way these rejection letters confirmed more explicitly than ever the curious formula the BBC had devised to justify excluding from its output anything which appeared to contradict the 'consensus'.

'BBC News currently takes the view', the letters ran, 'that their reporting needs to be calibrated to take into account the scientific consensus that global warming is man-made'. In order 'to avoid bias', the BBC Editorial Guidelines now said that all its coverage must conform with 'mainstream science'. To allow airtime to those differing from the mainstream would only give audiences a false impression by implying that 'the argument was evenly balanced'. In the name of avoiding bias, therefore, the BBC was thus ruling that its coverage should be as biased as possible.

A month later there followed another striking example of how far those in positions of influence in British life had become carried away by groupthink, the practical implications of which were immeasurably more serious. This was an extraordinary event which took place that October in the House of Commons.

Back in 2005, when David Cameron became Conservative leader, looking for new policies which could show his party 'going green', a young woman called Bryony Worthington, the climate campaign director for Friends of the Earth, saw her opportunity. She suggested that his party should propose a radical new 'climate change law', which would commit Britain, uniquely in the world, to cutting its carbon dioxide emissions by 60 percent.[51]

By 2007 Labour's environment secretary David Miliband had got wind of this and, still carried away by his excitement over the IPCC's latest report, he did not wish to be politically outflanked. He first invited Ms Worthington to join his department, to advise on 'climate change education', and then invited her to play a leading role in drafting the legislation needed to put her proposal into law.

By 2008 the resulting Climate Change Bill, to commit Britain by 2050 to cutting its 'carbon emissions' by 60 percent of their 1990 level was going through Parliament, virtually without opposition. It had already been through two of its three readings when Miliband was promoted to become foreign secretary. His brother Ed Miliband was put in charge of a new ministry, the Department of Energy and Climate Change, and it was he who came to the Commons on 29 October to pilot the Bill through its third reading. At the last minute he was talked, by Worthington and others, into amending the Bill to raise its carbon dioxide reduction target to 80 percent.

It was evident from the scores of speeches through a six-hour debate that not a single MP had the faintest idea of how in practice such a target could be met. This was simply not discussed, even though in reality it could only be achieved by closing down virtually the whole of Britain's fossil-fuel-dependent economy.

Only two MPs questioned the need for such a law at all, and only one, the former Conservative Cabinet minister Peter Lilley, raised the matter of its cost. Based on the original 60 percent target, this had been estimated by the government at £205 billion, which would make it far and away the most expensive law ever passed through Parliament.

But its estimate of the benefits flowing from the Bill was only £110 billion. In other words, MPs were being asked to vote for a Bill which even the government's own figures showed would cost almost twice as much as any benefits it might bring. And because the change from 60 to 80 percent had only been made at the last minute, no cost–benefit estimate for the new target was yet available.

Just before the final vote was taken, Lilley drew to the House's attention that, outside in Parliament Square, snow was falling, the first known in London in October for 74 years. Their heads filled only with the happy belief that they were doing their bit to save the planet from runaway global warming, 463 MPs voted for the Bill. Only five voted against. Not one of the MPs who had now voted, all-but unanimously, for by far the most costly piece of legislation in British history could have begun to explain how its aims might be achieved, except by shutting down Britain's economy. It was an overwhelming example of the power of collective make-believe.

Even if Britain did reduce its carbon dioxide emissions by more than four-fifths within 42 years, this would not have the slightest effect on total global emissions, to which Britain was by now contributing only 1.6 percent, at a time when China was adding more than this to the total every year.

Only five months later did the government publish its revised cost-benefit analysis for meeting the new 80 percent target. This showed that the cost of the Climate Change Act might now be £404 billion, nearly twice the original estimate, averaging out at up to £18 billion every year until 2050 (equivalent to £720 a year for every household in the land). But the new figure for the benefits of the Act was now calculated to have risen nearly tenfold to £1,024 billion. It then emerged that the government's reason for this was that most of these benefits were not to be enjoyed by the people of Britain themselves but by the world as a whole.

In every respect, because of the unimaginable scale of its implications, this legislation had shown Britain's politicians having been led into a collective flight from reality greater than any that can be recalled in the country's history.

Climategate and Copenhagen

> The more amiability and esprit de corps among the members of a policy-making in-group, the greater is the danger that independent critical thinking will be replaced by groupthink, which is likely to result in irrational and dehumanised actions directed towards out-groups.
>
> Irving Janis, Introduction to *Groupthink*

> The fact is that we can't account for the lack of warming at the moment, and it is a travesty that we can't.
>
> Kevin Trenberth email to Michael Mann, 9 October 2009

Those British politicians were not alone. Just when the Climate Change Act was being passed, the world was entering another freezing winter, in a year which had begun with record snowfalls across the Northern Hemisphere. In the US the early months of 2008 had caused it to be known as 'the winter from hell'. There had been unfamiliar snow and cold even in Saudi Arabia and the deserts of Iran. By 2009 it was ten years since global temperatures had shown any warming trend.

But preparations were now in full swing for the next great UNFCCC conference, in Copenhagen in December 2009, to agree a new treaty to halt global warming much more stringent than the Kyoto Protocol it was intended to replace.

For months in the run-up to Copenhagen the Western media ran with a flow of stories on new scientific studies purporting to show that the consequences of global warming were now 'even worse than previously predicted'. But on November 19, out of the blue, came the anonymous release across the internet of more than 1000 emails and 3000 other documents from the database of the University of East Anglia's CRU. These shed such damaging light on the activities of the little group of scientists at the heart of the IPCC that what they revealed was almost immediately dubbed 'Climategate'.

The Climategate files reflected the three key ingredients of groupthink: the shakiness of its relation to factual evidence; the crucial need therefore to preserve the illusion of a 'consensus'; and how this then leads to what Janis called the 'irrational and dehumanised' hostility displayed to anyone daring to challenge it.

They revealed for a start the tortuous lengths to which these scientists at the heart of the 'consensus' had been prepared to go in manipulating the data to support their 'narrative'; most conspicuously in the case of using 'Mike's *Nature* trick' to 'hide the decline'. In addition, the CRU's computer files were shown to be in a chaotic state, and many had been 'lost'.

But the emails then showed the remarkable degree of hostility towards anyone who disagreed with them. Polite requests for background data that might explain how particular conclusions had been arrived at were flatly refused, on the grounds that this would only be used to undermine those conclusions.[52] When, in 2008, yet another request for data had been put in to CRU, this time under the Freedom of Information Act, Jones warned the little circle of scientists that, in breach of FOI law, they should delete hundreds of emails that might be potentially embarrassing.[53]

These tiresome outsiders, and particularly the critics of the 'hockey stick', had to be silenced or discredited by any available means. This applied not only to McIntyre but also to Soon and Baliunas[†] and also to John Daly, who, even before McIntyre published his analysis of the computer tricks used to compile his graph, had separately published a weight of other scientific evidence to confirm that the Medieval Warm Period had indeed existed. When Daly died in Australia in 2004, Jones emailed Mann to say that the news of his death was 'cheering'.

The emails revealed the efforts the group had made to keep any papers dissenting from the 'consensus' out of the scientific journals. In the case of those journals that had published the Soon/Baliunas and McIntyre/McKitrick papers, they had discussed ways whereby either their editors might be ejected from their posts, or that the journal itself might somehow be ostracised by the scientific community.

Finally, one of the last of the emails in October 2009 (quoted above) showed how frustrated the little group had become by their inability to explain why global temperatures were no longer continuing to rise as their models had predicted. This was Trenberth's plaintive admission that it was a 'travesty' that 'we can't account for the lack of warming'.

Just a fortnight after Climategate first burst into the headlines, politicians representing 180 countries, led by President Barack Obama, joined 100,000 other people in Copenhagen, including officials, scientists, green pressure groups, climate activists and commercial lobbyists seeking to exploit the ever-growing bonanza of subsidies available to investors in 'low-carbon' projects. It was the largest international conference since Rio in 1992.

But, as inches of snow fell on the freezing city outside, the atmosphere in the mammoth conference venue became ever more heated, fractious and despondent. For reasons that might have been predicted as far back as Kyoto, the new global treaty that had been planned for so long was just not going to happen. There was never going to be agreement on a deal even more one-sided than Kyoto. On one hand the new treaty would have committed the 'Annex 1' Western countries not only to making drastic cuts in their carbon dioxide emissions but at the same time to pay out hundreds of billions of dollars to the 'developing' Annex 2 nations to assist them in moving towards 'low-carbon' economies. On the other, those developing nations, led by China and India, might be happy enough to accept the money. But in no way would they agree to curbing their own emissions in return.

From a fortnight of bitter wrangling, little more emerged than agreement that they should all meet again in a few years' time to have another go: Copenhagen was a fiasco. Groupthink might have led them all to agree on the righteousness of their cause, but when this ran up against hard economic realities, it was shown to have been no more than a colossal act of collective wishful-thinking.

† See p. 24.

14 Where did the 'consensus' get its 'facts'?

> The IPCC studies only peer-reviewed science.
>
> Dr Rajendra Pachauri, chairman of the IPCC, 1 November 2009.[54]

In the space of just a few weeks, the hitherto seemingly impregnable fortress of the 'consensus' had been dealt two hammer blows. The failure of Copenhagen was impossible to hide, although the BBC's chief environment correspondent Richard Black managed, on the BBC's website, to ascribe the blame for it on eight different factors, ranging from the EU and President Obama's distraction by US television schedules to the snow falling on the conference centre. But he omitted to mention the one overriding reason why its failure had long been wholly predictable. The real significance of Climategate was widely missed by the media, not least because so few journalists were aware just how far the little group of scientists responsible for the emails had been, more than any others, responsible for promoting the global warming cause at the heart of the IPCC establishment. But, in the weeks that followed, for a very different reason, the IPCC itself became the focus of a series of revelations which threatened more than anything before to undermine its authority.

Both the IPCC and its supporters had long made no more insistent claim than that it relied only on 'peer-reviewed science': on papers which had supposedly been approved by other independent experts in the field as being soundly based and credible. In fact, a study in 2008 of the key chapter in the 2007 report on 'understanding and attributing climate change' showed that it had been written by just 53 authors, of whom 60 percent came from research units in the US and Britain that were firmly committed to the 'consensus' cause (including no fewer than ten from the Hadley Centre). Most had co-authored papers with each other or favourably 'peer-reviewed' each other's work.[55] When the media and politicians spoke reverentially of IPCC reports as being the work of '1500 climate scientists', it was in essence only these 53 they were referring to, because everything else in those reports was meant to depend on their findings.

But now a series of detailed investigations brought to light something even more unexpected about the sources the 2007 report had drawn on to support some of its most widely-publicised claims. Many of these, it turned out (all from Working Group II on the 'impacts of climate change'), had not been based on peer-reviewed research at all. They had been taken from propaganda material put out by climate activists and environmental pressure groups. In fact, the first of these scandals, dubbed 'Glaciergate', had begun to break two days before the Copenhagen conference opened. It was reported from Delhi that the Indian government had commissioned the country's most respected glaciologist, Dr Vijay Raina, to look into the 2007 report's startling claim that Himalayan glaciers were retreating so fast that, by 2035, most could have disappeared. When Raina stated that this prediction had no scientific foundation whatever, Dr Pachauri responded that his opinion was 'voodoo science', and stood by the IPCC's claim.

But it wasn't until January 2010 that there emerged the full story of where this prediction originated. It had first appeared in an interview given to a small environmental magazine in 1999 by an obscure glaciologist, Dr Syed Hasnain. From there it had been quoted in 2005 by the WWF, and it was this group that the IPCC cited as its source. Even before the report was finalised, an IPCC lead author, Dr George Kaser, had apparently dismissed the prediction as 'so wrong that it is not even worth discussing'. But it was published anyway. It also emerged that in 2008 Pachauri had appointed Hasnain to head a new glaciology unit at his TERI institute in Delhi.[56]

Next to come to light, as 'Amazongate', were the origins of another of the 2007 report's most widely-publicised claims: that global warming was threatening to destroy 40 percent of the Amazon rainforest. Again the WWF had been cited as the source, but in fact the '40 percent' figure had first appeared in a propaganda leaflet produced in 1999 by a little Brazilian environmental group linked to the WWF. And even here, the '40 percent' prediction had not been attributed to global warming at all, but to damage being done by logging and man-made fires.

This was then followed by 'Africagate', centred on another widely quoted prediction: that droughts caused by global warming could by 2050 lead to a halving of African crop yields. This turned out to have been sourced to a single paper by a Moroccan academic, who claimed that he had based it on reports for three North African governments. But none of these had in fact said anything of the kind. One had even forecast that crop yields might actually rise.

Each of these three claims had not only been highlighted in Pachauri's Summary for Policymakers, but were among the most widely quoted in the media coverage given to the report. The BBC had immediately given them pride of place on its website, in a guide to 'Climate change around the world'.

The resulting stir prompted a diligent Canadian journalist, Donna Laframboise, to invite readers of her blog to co-operate in checking out every single source given for statements in the 2007 report. Her 40-strong team discovered that, of the 18,531 scientific references cited in the report, no fewer than 5,587, nearly a third, had not been peer-reviewed academic studies at all, but were 'newspaper and magazine articles, discussion papers, MA and PhD theses, working papers and advocacy literature published by environmental groups'.[57]

No one had more often been quoted as insisting that the IPCC reports relied only on unimpeachable 'peer-reviewed science' than Pachauri himself. However, it was further revealed that, thanks to the worldwide prestige he enjoyed as IPCC chairman, he had been able to expand his little Delhi research institute, TERI, into quite an empire, with branches in Washington, London, Abu Dhabi and several countries in south-east Asia. He had also been given advisory positions with more than 20 organisations, ranging from world-ranking international banks and corporations, to two carbon trading exchanges benefiting from the multi-billion dollar trade in buying and selling 'carbon credits', and finally to several universities, including Yale, which appointed Pachauri to head its new Climate and Energy Institute.

Pachauri, famous in India for his $1,000 suits and his expensive home in the most exclusive residential enclave in Delhi, was quick to protest that none of all the money given for his advisory services was paid to him personally, but had all gone to his institute.[58] In recent years however, the head of the IPCC had cut an increasingly eccentric figure, as when he called for the world to give up eating meat, because the methane given off by the digestive system of farm animals made as great a contribution to global warming as all the world's transport. Naturally, when details of his wide-ranging commercial activities were revealed, no one was quicker to leap to his defence than the BBC, which published a laudatory profile. But this failed to give any details of the startling expansion of his TERI empire, or the impressive array of organisations which had paid for his services.

Not all the efforts of Pachauri's allies to defend him, however, could obscure the fact that the extraordinary prestige previously accorded to the IPCC had for the first time been very seriously dented. The question now was: how would the 'consensus' establishment defuse the crisis?

15 Groupthink defends its own

The inquiries into Climategate and the IPCC

> It is especially important that, despite the deluge of allegations and smears against the CRU, this independent group of utterly reputable scientists have concluded that there was no evidence of any scientific malpractice.
>
> Edward Acton, vice-chancellor of the University of East Anglia, on the Oxburgh report into Climategate emails, 14 April 2010

There was no doubt that the 'climate establishment' was badly winded by the double-whammy of Climategate and the scandalous revelations about the IPCC. In February 2010 Phil Jones temporarily stepped down as director of the CRU, and said that he had 'several times' thought about committing suicide. A few days later, when he was interviewed by the BBC, Roger Harrabin very unusually let it be known that some of the questions he wanted to ask had been suggested to him by 'climate sceptics'.

This led to Jones's startling admission that, since 1995, there had been 'no statistically significant global warming'; and furthermore that the rate of warming in earlier years, between 1860 and1880 and 1910 and 1940, had been 'not statistically different' from that between 1975 and 2009.[59]

But this apart, it did not take long for the authorities to mount a classic establishment response to the crisis. No fewer than eight separate official inquiries were launched into Climategate, five in America and three in Britain, one by the Commons Science and Technology Committee, the other two by the University of East Anglia itself.

First to report were the MPs, all but one of whom seemed to be firmly lined up with the 'consensus', as indeed did almost all the witnesses they interviewed.[60] Unsurprisingly, the MPs reported that 'the scientific reputation of Professor Jones and CRU remains intact'. The emails did not 'challenge the consensus that global warming is happening and is induced by human activity'. There was no reason why Professor Jones should not resume his post.

The members of the second inquiry to report, known as the 'Independent Science Assessment Committee' and set up by the UEA, were again almost entirely firm supporters of the 'consensus'. It was chaired by Lord Oxburgh, who had various financial interests in 'low carbon' energy, including his presidency of the Carbon Capture and Storage Association. He was also a member of GLOBE, a shadowy international body set up to co-ordinate efforts to push the 'consensus' cause by members of an array of national parliaments.

Oxburgh's inquiry seemed a curiously perfunctory affair. Its researches involved only two brief interviews of Jones, and examination of ten mostly uncontroversial papers, almost certainly chosen by Jones himself. Again, its brief report found 'no evidence of any deliberate scientific malpractice' and that the CRU's work had been 'carried out with integrity'. Jones's team had been 'objective and dispassionate in their view of the data and their results'. There was 'no hint of tailoring the results to a particular agenda'. 'Their sole aim' had been 'to establish as robust a record of temperatures in recent centuries as possible'.

The third inquiry, the 'Independent Climate Change Email Review', also set up by the UEA, was chaired by Sir Muir Russell, a former senior civil servant, now vice-chancellor of Glasgow University. It did not report until July 2010, and again found that the 'rigour and honesty' of the CRU scientists were not in doubt. They had not tried to suppress criticism; and the key data needed to replicate their findings had always been freely available to any 'competent' scientist. No sooner was this report published than Jones returned to his post.

The only seriously dissenting voice on any of these panels had been that of a Labour member of the Commons committee, Graham Stringer, a trained scientist who, before becoming an MP, had worked as an analytical chemist. Following the other two inquiries, he wrote a minority report to say that the serious issues raised by the Climategate emails should have merited 'independent and objective scrutiny by independent panels. This has not happened'.

'No reputable scientist who was critical of the CRU's work' had been on either of the scientific panels; and 'prominent and distinguished critics were not interviewed'. These and other failings had left 'a question mark against whether CRU science is reliable'. The Oxburgh panel had not looked at the 'CRU's controversial work on the IPCC, which is what has attracted most serious allegations'. 'Russell did not investigate the deletion of emails.' All in all, Stringer concluded, 'we are now left without a clear understanding of whether or not the CRU science is compromised'.

But that, of course, had been the whole purpose of the exercise: to avoid focussing on any of the real key points at issue, to ensure that the scientists were cleared of any serious criticism, and to produce reports which could then be quoted by supporters of the 'consensus' (as indeed they very widely were), to show that the entire Climategate furore had been found by 'independent experts' to be just a fuss about nothing. And, in keeping with the principles of groupthink, Stringer's fellow MPs ruled, very exceptionally, that his dissenting comments should be excluded from their final report.[61]

Less obviously one-sided in terms of damage limitation was the response of the international scientific establishment to the flaws brought to light in the IPCC's 2007 report. Indeed, so blatantly incorrect was its prediction about the disappearing Himalayan glaciers that the IPCC itself had already withdrawn it. But the main task of investigating the IPCC was given to a panel set up by the Interacademy Council, representing 15 of the world's leading scientific bodies. These included the US National Academy of Sciences and Britain's Royal Society.

When this panel reported in August 2010, it did identify a good many failings in how the IPCC was run, recommending significant changes. The process of ensuring that scientific sources were properly peer-reviewed should be tightened up. Indeed, the panel had even carried out its own analysis of those cited in the Third Assessment Report of 2001. This found that only 84 percent of papers cited by Working Group I had been peer-reviewed. The figure for Working Group II was even lower, just 50 percent. That for Working Group III was a mere 30 percent.

The report also recommended a reorganisation of the IPCC's top management structure, with a clear hint that Pachauri himself should stand down. But this was not to happen until

February 2015, for reasons wholly unconnected with the IPCC.[62]

At least it was likely that the IPCC's fifth report, due to appear in 2014, would not repeat the more glaring mistakes which had been so embarrassing in its two predecessors. In this respect, at least the 'consensus' was learning to be rather more cautious.

16 Aftermath of the crisis, 2010–2014

The story now enters a new phase. In 22 years it had risen to two climaxes. The first, between 2005 and 2007, was the time when the propaganda claims made for the 'consensus' had been at their most reckless, as in Gore's film and the IPCC's 2007 report. The second came in the winter of 2009/10, when the 'consensus' for the first time ran into real difficulties, with Climategate, Copenhagen and the exposing of the errors in that same IPCC report.

Over the next five years, between 2010 and 2014, the story was to unfold in a markedly lower key. At a series of lacklustre annual UNFCCC conferences in Cancun, Durban, Doha, Warsaw and Lima, the climate establishment laboriously tried to salvage something from the wreckage of Copenhagen, attempting to devise some formula whereby the aborted treaty could be revived. The target for this was a new mega-conference planned for Paris in 2015. Meanwhile, in 2014, the IPCC's Fifth Assessment Report was noticeably more restrained in its claims than any of its predecessors.

But we now look at some of the ways in which, during these years, supporters of the 'consensus' tried to keep their cause alive, still exemplifying each of the three rules of groupthink.

Janis's Rule 1: failure to connect with reality

A major problem for the 'consensus' by this time was the continued failure of global temperatures to rise as its computer models had predicted. Even the IPCC recognised what had become known as 'the pause'. All the official data still showed 1998 to have been the warmest year in recent times, since when, allowing for fluctuations up and down, there had been no trend at all.

Against this background, one of the more significant tactics used to suggest that the impacts of global warming were still getting worse was to claim that it was causing a marked increase in floods, droughts, heatwaves and hurricanes. It was also said that there were other signs that the world's climate system was becoming 'more chaotic'.

Those 'extreme weather events' we'd seen before

This game had, of course, been played previously, as with the 2003 European heatwave and the Hurricane Katrina disaster in 2005. On each occasion it was widely claimed that such events were now becoming more frequent and intense, although neither in fact had yet been repeated. Since 2005 Atlantic hurricane activity had been at its lowest level for decades, and although 2003 had seen the hottest day ever recorded in Britain, that summer had been nothing like the months of prolonged heat experienced in the drought year of 1976.

But 2010 brought a rash of further 'extreme weather events', each claimed to have been 'unprecedented', from a heatwave in western Russia to disastrous floods in Pakistan and Queensland. These were all seized on as further evidence of 'dangerous climate change'. Referring to each of these examples in July 2011, the British government's chief scientific adviser, Sir John Beddington, a population biologist, proposed that politicians should 'use such climate-related disasters overseas to persuade British voters to accept unpopular policies for curbing carbon emissions'.[63] He was clearly unaware that a paper in *Geophysical Research Letters* had already demonstrated that no significant warming trend could be discerned in that part of Russia over the previous 130 years. Similar studies had pointed out that, far from the floods in Pakistan and Queensland being unprecedented, significantly worse had been experienced, in Pakistan in 1929 and in Queensland in 1974.[64]

Beddington also referred to a more recent drought in the Horn of Africa, described as 'the worst for 60 years'. Unfortunately, the IPCC's 2007 report had predicted that, due to climate change, that region would in future get wetter.

In October 2012 there was much excitement among politicians and the media over 'Hurricane Sandy', as it turned upwards from the Caribbean towards the north-eastern US coast. This was forecast as likely to generate an 'unprecedented storm surge', thanks to ocean warming and rising sea levels caused by climate change. In fact, by the time 'Sandy' made US landfall, it had weakened to only a Force 1 extra-tropical storm; and historical records showed that the New England coast had experienced seven greater storm surges in the past, all before 1960 and going back to 1635.

Even pillars of the climate establishment were becoming wary of ascribing 'extreme weather events' to climate change. In 2013 an editorial in *Nature* pronounced that 'better models are needed before exceptional events can be reliably linked to global warming'. A 'Special Report on Extremes' published by the IPCC the same year similarly concluded that there was 'high agreement' that 'long-term trends' in extreme weather events could not be 'attributed to natural or anthropogenic climate change'.[65]

How that 'vanishing Arctic ice' failed to vanish

There was no more conspicuous example of the way groupthink is unable to recognise any evidence that contradicts its chosen narrative than the obsessive attention that had been given to the state of ice in the Arctic (along with the supposedly threatened survival of those, in fact, non-disappearing polar bears).

Satellite measurements since 1979 had recorded an overall declining trend in the extent to which the ice was melting in late summer. Two professors, Wieslaw Malowski in California and Peter Wadhams of Cambridge, had been in the forefront of warning, on the basis of computer models, that, after its summer melt, the Arctic would soon be 'ice free'.

When in September 2007 the ice shrank to its lowest point yet, they predicted that the ice would all be gone 'by 2013'. The following July, the *Independent* devoted its entire front page to announcing that this could happen by September that year. But it was just then that the ice began a dramatic recovery.[66] By the end of summer 2012 the ice-melt again broke the record, with the remaining ice thinner than ever. Wadhams now predicted that it would all be gone 'by

2016'. But by 2014 measurements made by the Danish Meteorological Institute (DMI) showed that the ice extent was not only back to where it had been in 2006, but had also thickened on average by 33 percent.

In June 2016 Wadhams was to publish a book entitled *Farewell to Ice*. Under such headlines as 'Arctic could be ice-free for first time in 100,000 years, claims leading scientist', he was quoted as predicting that by that September it could have shrunk to an area of 'less than 1 million square kilometres'. But by 10 September, when the ice began re-freezing at its earliest date since daily records began in 1987, its smallest extent had been 4.1 million square kilometres. This was more than four times larger than Wadhams' prediction.

Yet again what the carbon dioxide-obsessed computer modellers failed to allow for were the natural factors that had brought about similar warming of the Arctic in the 1930s. This resulted from warm water pushing up into the Arctic, the result of a shift in the Atlantic Multidecadal Oscillation, which had correlated before with fluctuations in Arctic sea temperatures.

Still more significantly, what the groupthinkers also consistently tried to ignore was that the relative decline in the extent of Arctic summer ice had been more than counter-balanced by the steady growth in both the extent and volume of sea ice in Antarctica, at the other end of the earth.[67] This meant that, by 2014, there was significantly more polar ice in the world than there had been at any time since satellite observations began in 1979. But wasn't the point about this 'warming' that it was meant to be 'global'?

Why the Met Office's Unified Model got it so wrong

Another body which attracted increasingly quizzical attention in these years was the UK Met Office. Few official institutions had played a greater part in evangelising for 'consensus' groupthink, ever since John Houghton, as a passionate convert to the belief in 'human-induced climate change', became its director back in the 1980s.

In 1990, when he was already the most influential figure at the top of the IPCC, Houghton, as we know, had set up the Hadley Centre for Climate Prediction, which, along with the University of East Anglia's CRU, was responsible for one of the two main official global surface temperature records. The predictions made by its computer models helped to play a very significant part in shaping the IPCC's reports.

In 2010 the Met Office's chief scientist, Julia Slingo, told the Commons Climategate inquiry that its new £33 million super-computer was not only responsible for predicting future global temperatures as far ahead as 2100, but also for its shorter-term weather forecasts for the UK.[68] This was what she proudly called the Met Office's 'Unified Model'. But even before 2010, its forecasts had become conspicuously unreliable. In 2004 the Hadley Centre produced a report entitled *Uncertainty, Risk and Dangerous Climate Change*. This predicted that over the next ten years, global temperatures would have risen by 0.3°C. Four of the five years after 2009 would be hotter than 1998. Not only would heatwaves like that in 2003 become more frequent, but by 2040 more than half of all European summers were 'likely to be warmer than that of 2003' and 'by the 2060s a 2003-type summer would be unusually cool'.[69]

In early 2007 global warming hysteria was at its height. The new chairman of the Met Office, Robert Napier, previously a director of the UK branch of WWF, was saying that it would be the 'warmest year ever'. This was just before global temperatures temporarily plummeted by 0.7°C. That summer in the UK, it forecast, it would be 'drier than average', just before some of the worst summer floods in living memory.

The Met Office's Unified Model consistently predicted 'hotter, drier summers' and 'warmer than average' winters for 2008–2010, three years when much of the Northern Hemisphere endured record winter cold and snow, and while the UK had summers that were wetter and cooler than usual. The Met Office's prediction of a 'barbecue summer' in 2009 was famously followed by three months of unusual rain. In October 2010 the Unified Model predicted that Britain's winter would be up to '2 degrees warmer than average', just before the coldest December since records began in 1659.

In late 2011 the Met Office website forecast that global temperatures would rise over the next five years by up to 0.5°C from their 1971–2000 average. This prediction was so embarrassingly off-beam that, only a year later, it was quietly removed from the website, replaced with one predicting that the flat-lining temperature trend since 1998 was 'likely to continue'. In March 2012 it forecast that Britain's spring would, yet again, be 'drier than average', just before the wettest April on record. In the autumn of 2013 it predicted that the winter months would be 'drier than average' just before the wettest three months for 84 years brought disastrous flooding to Somerset and the Thames Valley.[70]

In 2014 it was finally possible to check on the accuracy of that ten-year forecast of global temperatures the Hadley Centre had made in 2004. Instead of the world having warmed by 0.3°C, as predicted, the temperature trend according to the satellite record had not risen at all. Far from four of the five years after 2009 having been hotter than 1998, this still stood as warmer than any year since.

Again, the chief reason why the Met Office's Unified Model had got it all so spectacularly wrong was that it was programmed to assume that the chief factor determining temperatures and climate was the continuing rise in carbon dioxide. Hence all those 'hotter, drier summers' and 'warmer than average' winters.

Yet so powerful was the mindset which had the Met Office in its grip that it could not recognise why it had made such a breathtaking series of errors. In its 2014 annual report, its new chairman announced that the Met Office was now buying a new £97 million super-computer, to replace their five-year-old £33 million version. This, he said, would not only enable their 'integrated weather and climate model, known as the Met Office's Unified Model' to 'produce the most accurate short-term forecasts that are scientifically possible'. It would also be able to predict even more accurately how the Earth's climate was likely to change over the next 100 years.

The extent to which, blinded by its obsession, the Met Office had so long continued to repeat such errors, should have become a national scandal. As a body costing the taxpayers £220 million a year, with its chief scientist alone receiving nearly £240,000, the politicians might have been expected to ask how it could claim to deserve this money. But so far from reality had the MPs themselves been carried by the same groupthink that the Met Office was allowed to carry on without ever being called to account.[71]

Janis's Rule 2: preserving the illusion of 'consensus'

With all the new problems which had arisen for the 'consensus' in recent years, it had become more than ever important to maintain the impression that virtually 'all the world's scientists' still believed that global warming was caused by human agency.

'97 percent of climate scientists believe in man-made global warming'

This need to assure the world that only an insignificant handful of scientists did not agree with the climate orthodoxy had already prompted a first response back in 2008, when the *Washington Post,* the *Guardian* and others trumpeted a new survey which had found that '97 percent of climate scientists' agreed with the 'consensus' on man-made warming. This was said to be based on questioning '10,257 Earth scientists'.

But when the evidence for this claim was looked into, it turned out not to be quite what all those headlines had suggested. For a start, the survey was the work of a master's degree student at the University of Illinois, under the guidance of her supervisor. She had indeed originally approached '10,257 Earth scientists', but it was then decided that many of these represented disciplines which did not qualify them to answer, including physicists, geologists, astronomers and experts on solar activity (who might have believed there was a connection between global warming and the Sun). So the original number of those approached was winnowed down to 3,146.

Those who remained were then asked two questions. First, did they accept that the world had warmed since the pre-industrial era. It might have been hard to find any reasonably well-informed person who disagreed with this, but even so 10 percent of them did so.

Secondly, did they believe that human activity had 'significantly' contributed to this warming'? When only 82 percent said they did, this was not considered to convey quite the required impression of an overwhelming 'consensus'. So the sample was winnowed down still further until the researchers were left with just 77 respondents who (a) described themselves as 'climate scientists' and (b) had recently published peer-reviewed papers on climate change. When 75 of the 77 gave the required answer to the second question, this provided the '97 percent' figure which won all those headlines (although it amounted to only 0.7 percent of the '10,257 earth scientists' originally approached).[72]

As these details emerged, they aroused so such mockery that in 2012 a group of highly committed advocates for the orthodoxy, including a journalist from the *Guardian*, decided to come to the rescue of the '97 percent' claim with what they called 'The Consensus Project'. The lead author of the paper which resulted was John Cook, an Australian with a PhD in psychology, who in 2011 had published a book called *Climate Change Denial: Heads In The Sand* and was co-founder of a blog called *Skeptical Science,* dedicated to 'getting sceptical about global warming skepticism'.

This time the team had searched the internet for the abstracts of papers published since 1991 that mentioned 'global climate change' or 'global warming'. Naturally it didn't occur to them to allow for the fact that the overwhelming majority of studies published during that time could only have won their funding if they endorsed the 'consensus' view. But their trawling produced 11,944 abstracts including those phrases, which they then divided into eight categories. These ranged from 'explicit endorsement with quantification' at the top, shading all the way down to 'explicit rejection with quantification' at the bottom.

7,980 of the abstracts expressed 'no position'. This left 34 percent of the papers still remaining. The overwhelming majority of these, 33 percent of the total, fell into one of the three categories which endorsed the belief that 'greenhouse gases lead to warming'. 33 percent of that 34 percent thus gave Cook and his colleagues the '97 percent' figure they wanted.

On closer examination, however, this claim began to look ever more curious. The vast majority of the abstracts included in the 33 percent figure consisted of (a) those that had only agreed that human emissions were making some 'unquantified' contribution to global warming; and (b) those that merely agreed that greenhouse gases in general contribute to warming 'without explicitly stating that humans are the cause'. These two categories were so vague that it would have been hard to disagree with either. But when it came to papers which fell into the top category, by 'explicitly' stating that 'human beings are the primary cause of recent global warming', these numbered only 65: just 1.6 percent of all those giving a position. Yet it was only by adding all these figures together that they could be translated into the claim that '97 percent of climate scientists agree on climate change' which made headlines around the world: not least when, on 16 May 2013, President Obama tweeted 'Ninety-seven percent of scientists agree climate change is real, man-made, dangerous'. The Cook paper had, of course, shown nothing of the kind. But a more accurate reflection of the survey's findings, that '1.6 percent of climate scientists agree that humans are the primary cause of global warming' would have won no coverage at all.

Obama was followed by his Secretary of State John Kerry, who used the '97 percent' finding to call for the American public to be 'pounding on the doors of Congress' to act: referring to 'global perils such as drought, floods, wildfires, threatened coastlines, disease risks and more', and adding 'the danger we face could not be more real.' And the '97 percent' figure continued to be quoted all over the place for years to come. Not since the 'hockey stick' had the believers in man-made warming been given such seemingly powerful evidence to support their cause.

If you don't support the 'consensus', you fail your exams

In few areas of life had the 'consensus' groupthink come to exercise a more commanding position than in Britain's education system, where almost an entire generation was now being instructed as if no view other than that the future of the planet was threatened by man-made climate change existed.

In April 2014, as a newspaper columnist, I was sent a General Studies paper set to A' Level students the previous year by the leading official exam body, AQA. Candidates were asked to discuss 11 pages of 'source materials' on climate change. These included excerpts from a whole set of documents, ranging from the IPCC's 2007 report to an article from the *Guardian*, all promoting the 'consensus' view.

One item quoted the Met Office predicting that 'even if global temperatures only rise by 2°C, 30–40 percent of species could face extinction'. A graph from the US Environmental Protection Agency showed temperatures having soared in the past century by 1.4°C, twice the generally accepted figure. The only hint that anyone in the world might question such statements was an article by an environmental correspondent for the *Daily Telegraph*, Louise Gray (who had previously worked for WWF). This quoted a paid PR man for the cause, Bob Ward of the Grantham Institute, dismissing 'climate sceptics' as 'a remnant group of dinosaurs' who 'misunderstood the point of science'.

In reporting all this I commented:

> In the days when one purpose of education was to teach people to examine the evidence and to think rationally, any bright student might have had a field day, showing how all these extracts were no more than one-sided propaganda. But today one fears they would have been marked down so severely for not coming up with the desired answers that they would have been among the tiny handful of candidates given an unequivocal 'fail'.

In response I had an email which could not have more vividly confirmed this. It came from the mother of just such a student, who she described as 'an excellent scientist' who had scored 'straight As' on all his science papers. But he was also 'very knowledgeable about climate change and very sceptical about man-made global warming'.

His answers to the General Studies paper, questioning the reliability of each of its source materials, were given an 'E', the lowest possible mark. This seemed so implausible that the mother paid £60 for his paper to be 'independently' re-marked. When his manuscript was returned it was found to have been 'articulate, well-structured and clearly well-informed'. But again he was marked down with an 'E' for fail. [73]

Until a decade or two earlier, it would have been unthinkable in Britain that such a capable boy would not have been given high marks for showing how he was bright enough to think for himself. But so rigid now was the grip the groupthink had come to exercise over Britain's education system that any student failing to parrot its mantras could expect to be given lower marks than anyone else in the class.

Janis's Rule 3: dissent from the 'consensus' can no longer be tolerated

We end this section with three more examples of how hostile advocates of the 'consensus' had now become to anyone outside the groupthink bubble. The first leads on neatly from that school exam paper because it also played on the pressure to enforce 'correct thinking' in Britain's schools.

Deniers must be 'eliminated'

One of the defining characteristics of groupthink, as Janis puts it, is that it is 'likely to result in irrational and dehumanised actions directed towards out-groups'. There could not have been a better unconscious illustration of this tendency than a little film launched in October 2010 for showing in Britain's cinemas and across the internet. *No Pressure* was made for 10:10, a campaign urging everyone in 2010 to cut their personal 'carbon footprint' by 10 percent.

The film's 'creator' was one of Britain's most successful comedy scriptwriters and directors, Richard Curtis, best-known for *Four Weddings and a Funeral, Notting Hill* and *Love Actually*, and as a co-founder of BBC televison's hugely popular annual fund-raising exercise for charity, *Comic Relief.*

The video opened with a gushing school teacher, played by a well-known actress, Gillian Anderson, telling her class that there was a 'brilliant idea' going round, that people should cut their 'carbon emissions by 10 percent', to keep 'the planet safe for everyone'. She asks the class what they might think of doing for the cause, particularly pleased with one girl who says she will be cycling to school instead of coming by car. 'Fantastic, Jemima!'.

'No pressure', the teacher gushes on, 'but it would be great to get an idea of how many of you are going to do this'. It seems as if every hand has been raised, until she notices that Philip and Tracy have refused to join in. Smiling on, she says 'absolutely fine, your own choice' and prepares to end the lesson – until she remembers something, 'Oh, just before you go', she says, reaching under the papers on her desk, 'I just need to press this button'. She does so and Philip and Tracy explode into fragments all around the room, showering blood and body parts over the desks and white shirts of their horrified fellow pupils.

Scene two, showing the equally ingratiating headmaster looking down on a hall-full of older pupils, is like a shorter repeat of scene one. Again, all the pupils except two raise their hands. Again, 'no pressure' and the button is pressed, again showering the other horrified students with blood. Scene three switches to David Ginola, then the well-known manager of Tottenham Hotspur (a football club which supported 10:10), on a practice pitch with his players. Again, when only he among his team shows no interest in cutting his 'carbon emissions', he is blown to smithereens.

No weirder advertisement for the 'consensus' cause had ever been devised. No sooner was it released than uproar broke out across the internet. Even many 'environmentalists' expressed shock and dismay, protesting that the film had gone way over the top. Within 24 hours it had been pulled off the air. Nevertheless, the *Guardian* did its best to defend the video, reporting that 'many people on our comment threads and Twitter thought the pantomime gore in the film was hilarious', and pointing out that at least it had won 'global' publicity for their cause. Indeed, all those involved in making the film must themselves have agreed that this was a really amusing way to put over their vital message. After all, 'deniers' were so dangerously mistaken on this central moral issue of our time that it could surely not be wrong to imagine them – of course only in a perfectly harmless, playful way – being literally wiped off the face of the earth.

The BBC attacks the 'deniers'

No British institution had been more relentless in pushing a propagandist line on all issues related to climate change than the BBC. Essentially its position was not dissimilar to that held by the makers of *No Pressure.* But in general its policy, as formalised after that 'secret seminar' in 2006, was that anyone or anything appearing to contradict the 'consensus' narrative should be rigorously ignored in its coverage. In 2010, however, after all the negative publicity recently given to the cause, the BBC decided that it was time once again to go on the attack against these 'deniers'. Among the results were the two remaining examples in this section.[74]

The first was a special hour-long edition of the BBC's flagship science programme, *Horizon*, entitled *Science Under Attack*, broadcast in January 2011. For their front-man they chose one of the chief figureheads of Britain's scientific establishment, Sir Paul Nurse, a molecular biologist, who was not only a Nobel prizewinner but also the new president of the Royal Society.

Nurse's case throughout the programme was that, although 'the vast majority of climate scientists' accepted man-made global warming, there were still 'deniers' or 'denialists' who refused to believe them. These people were now dangerously leading the public to lose trust in science (Nurse cited a poll finding that 50 percent of US voters now disbelieved in anthropogenic warming).

The programme's first aim therefore was to show the 'deniers' as being wholly without credibility, which it did by means of a technique already familiar from *Climate Wars*. This was to film interviews with two 'deniers', Dr Fred Singer and the journalist James Delingpole, who had first popularised the term Climategate, until brief clips could be extracted which, shown out of context, could be used to make them look ridiculous.

Dr Singer, the distinguished and ageing atmospheric physicist, was filmed chatting with Nurse in a New York diner, until he offered one example of the kind of evidence which seemed to confirm that solar activity had more influence on climate than carbon dioxide. He referred to data from stalagmites in 'a cave in the Arabian peninsula'. 'A cave in the Arabian peninsula?' Bingo! Nurse had just the clip he wanted.

This immediately cut to a sequence in which Nurse loftily contrasted Singer's single eccentric example with the way proper scientists like to look at all the data on a subject, to get an overall picture, instead of just 'cherry picking' one example on which to base some peculiar theory.[75]

Nurse then demonstrated what he meant by proper science by interviewing a computer-modeller from NASA, who waved aside any idea that solar activity could have been a 'primary factor' in recent warming by saying that this simply did not 'match up with evidence'. But then, in the most revealing passage in the programme, Nurse asked his NASA expert to quantify the relative contributions of carbon dioxide to the atmosphere by human and natural causes. The reply was that human activity was now emitting '7 gigatonnes of carbon dioxide' each year. But only '1 gigatonne' was emitted by the oceans, volcanoes and all other natural sources.

This answer seemed so extraordinary that Nurse asked him to repeat his claim that human emissions were now seven times greater than emissions from all natural sources put together. In reality, of course, this was a truly remarkable claim, since it is generally agreed that the total amount of carbon dioxide annually emitted into the atmosphere is not eight gigatonnes but some 186 gigatonnes. Of this, 100 gigatonnes (57 percent) is given off by the oceans, and 71 gigatonnes (38 percent) by animals. The 7 gigatonnes emitted by human activity thus represent not seven-eighths of the total but barely 3 percent.

But Nurse had got just the statistic he wanted even though, as baldly put to his viewers, it could not have been more ludicrously misleading. In fact, as elsewhere in the programme, Nurse gave little sign that he understood very much about climate science at all (as when at one point he said that he had 'read somewhere' that the planet had warmed by 0.7°C in the past century). The only real effort made to justify his title, *Science Under Attack*, was a sequence defending the CRU at East Anglia (the university Nurse himself had attended) over the Climategate emails.

This he did by allowing Professor Jones to explain why it had been entirely legitimate for the CRU to 'hide the decline' by the 'trick' used to get its temperature graph to show the 'hockey stick' shape that was wanted. On this and everything else revealed by the emails, as Nurse was quick to emphasise, four 'independent' enquiries had 'found no evidence of deliberate scientific malpractice'.

The real message of the programme was how it exemplified another familiar feature of the global warming 'debate'. This was the striking disparity between the unquestioning deference generally accorded to any scientists speaking for the 'consensus', and the very different treatment given to anyone who could be dismissed as just, to quote the Wikipedia entry on Dr Singer, 'an advocate for climate denial'.[76]

It was particularly noticeable how useful to the 'consensus' were scientists, like Nurse, holding some senior post in the scientific establishment. They could lend the 'prestige' of their position to the cause, even though their own scientific expertise all too often gave them no authority to do so. Just as this was so evident in Nurse's programme, so had it been in the bizarre pronouncements on climate issues by his predecessor as president of the Royal Society, the population biologist Lord May. May had also been a chief scientific adviser to the government, where he was succeeded by Sir David King, the surface chemist, and Sir John Beddington, another population biologist. Away from their own fields of expertise, as each of these men had abundantly demonstrated, they had no professional qualifications to pronounce on climate science whatever. Yet, thanks solely to the prestige attaching to their positions, they could each be used to propagandise for the groupthink party line as what Lenin liked to describe as 'useful idiots'.

The BBC tells itself that it needs 'more bias', not less

Later that year there followed as bizarre an example of the power of groupthink to invert reality as any described in these pages. Because there had been so much talk of 'BBC bias', the BBC Trust, its governing body, had commissioned an 'independent' report on *The Impartiality and Accuracy of the BBC's Coverage of Science*. The man chosen to write this was Professor Steve Jones, another geneticist, with a special interest in snails, who had also worked often for the BBC. Although only seven pages of Jones's 102-page report were devoted to the BBC's coverage of climate change, it became clear from its advance publicity, under headlines such as 'Sceptics get too much air-time, BBC told', that this was its key message. And it turned out that this was indeed the most important of Jones' findings: that the BBC had been giving too much coverage to 'climate deniers' and should in future keep them off the air. This was bizarre, since the essence of the BBC's policy had so long been to give those dissenting from the 'consensus' as little airtime as possible, and certainly they should never be given the opportunity to explain properly the reasons why they disagreed with it.

Jones made no secret of his own views, repeatedly talking of 'denialism', 'denialists' and 'deniers'. He described those outside the 'consensus' as a 'deluded minority', whose views were similar to those of astrologers, believers in alternative medicine, and even those who held that the 9/11 attack on the Twin Towers had been 'a US government plot'.

Other features of his report were even more surprising. One was how little Jones seemed to know about the BBC's coverage of climate issues. He referred only to a handful of programmes and the little he said about even these suggested that he had relied on a briefing supplied by others rather than having watched them himself.

In criticising the BBC's readiness to 'give space' to 'deniers' to make statements which 'are not supported by the facts', he mentioned as examples *Earth: Climate Wars* and *Science Under Attack*. He seemed unaware that the reason why they had been featured in those programmes was not to let them explain their views but to subject them to a hatchet job.

Jones was equally casual about his facts in referring to various recent controversies in the climate story. He poured scorn, for instance, on how 'deniers' had used 'a single mention in a report about Himalayan glaciers' as evidence of 'a conspiracy to exaggerate the impact of greenhouse gases'. This seemed an odd way to describe the huge row which had arisen over just one of the serious errors discovered in the IPCC's 2007 report, one which even the IPCC itself had realised was so indefensible that it had withdrawn the passage.

Jones seemed similarly hazy over the facts when he claimed that a survey of 'thousands of earth scientists' had shown that '97 percent of specialists in atmospheric physics' agreed that human activity played a significant part in causing global warming.

Almost the only aspect of Jones's report which perhaps should not have been surprising were various technical errors of his own, such as his misunderstanding of the debate over climate 'feedbacks', which showed how completely unfamiliar he was with even the basics of climate science.

But naturally, both the BBC Trust and the BBC Executive welcomed his 'key findings that our coverage of science is impartial, accurate and of high quality'. When it came to apportioning 'due weight' to different views, they agreed that there might be a case for tightening up the editorial guidelines still further. In other words, the BBC authorities agreed that, far from their coverage of climate change being biased, it should perhaps, in the name of 'impartiality', be made even more so. Not for nothing had George Orwell based his 'Ministry of Truth' in *Nineteen Eighty-Four* on his time working for the BBC.[77]

In the years between 2011 and 2014, as the temperature 'pause' continued, so the temperature of the debate over climate had become much less obviously feverish than in the previous decade. The IPCC's noticeably more restrained Fifth Assessment Report, published in dribs and drabs between 2013 and 2014, attracted significantly less media coverage than any of its predecessors. Despite storm Sandy in 2012 and the storms and floods in the UK in January 2014, much of the heat had also gone out of efforts to stoke up alarm over 'extreme weather events'.

But attention was now beginning to turn to the UNFCCC's next mammoth climate conference, planned for Paris in December 2015. Here it was hoped that the nations of the world would at last succeed in signing a new version of that binding treaty they had so signally failed to agree on at Copenhagen in 2009. As the fateful date approached, however, there was another highly revealing episode which, but for the all-pervading groupthink, should have attracted much more widespread attention than it did.

17 Prelude to Paris: 'adjusting' the facts to fit the theory (again)

When the facts change, I change my mind. What do you do, sir?

Apocryphally attributed to John Maynard Keynes

Apocryphal though this remark often attributed to Keynes may have been, it does completely reverse one of the common characteristics of groupthink. With groupthink, it is the belief that remains unshakeably the same. If anything needs to be changed, as we saw with the 'hockey stick', it has to be the facts.

It was no coincidence that in January 2015, with ten months to go before the Paris conference, a flurry of exultant headlines proclaimed that 2014 had been 'the hottest year on record'. From *Scientific American* and *Time* to the BBC and the *Guardian*, it was reported that startling new figures from the two most prominent global surface temperature records showed that 2014 had been even warmer than 1998. To understand the background to this we must recall that the main official records of global temperatures were derived from two different sources. Some are based on readings from thermometers situated on land and at sea. Others are based on readings from a global network of satellites and weather balloons. As we know, the two leading surface records were Gistemp, published by GISS, and HadCRUt, jointly compiled by the UK Met Office's Hadley Centre and Professor Jones' CRU. Both were of course prepared by leading advocates for the 'consensus'.[78] Of the two satellite records, one came from a department of the University of Alabama, Huntsville, run by Roy Spencer and John Christy, both 'climate sceptics', and the other from a company contracted to NASA, Remote Sensing Systems (RSS).

Until 1998, the surface and satellite records had remained generally in step with each other, but since then they had increasingly diverged. The surface records had consistently shown temperatures that were running rather higher than the satellites. Since 1998 GISS, in particular, had shown the temperature trend continuing to rise. But the satellite record, on the other hand, showed the trend flat-lining. Long before 2014 there had been puzzlement over this divergence between the surface and satellite records.

One factor which might have helped to account for it, analysed in detail by McIntyre, Anthony Watts and others, was that, in the years after 1990, there had been a dramatic drop in the number of weather stations on which the global surface record was based (from more than 6000 to fewer than 1500). Of the much smaller number of stations which remained, a much higher proportion were sited in built-up areas or at airports, where their data would be affected by the 'urban heat island' effect (which other studies had shown could result in temperatures up to 1°C or more higher than those in rural areas). Furthermore, over 80 percent of the earth's surface, including vast areas of Russia, Africa, Canada, Antarctica and 90 percent of the oceans, were not covered by instrumental readings at all.[79]

The satellite coverage on the other hand was significantly more comprehensive. Not only did it cover the entire globe, but it also constantly took readings at different levels of the atmosphere (hence the finding that there was no evidence for that IPCC-predicted 'fingerprint' of warming in the upper troposphere).

In January 2015 the puzzlement over the divergence of the surface and satellite records increased, with that rash of reports claiming that 2014 was now 'the hottest year' on record. This was because the satellite records were still showing 1998 as significantly warmer than any year since. This was the greatest divergence between the surface and satellite records so far.

But it then emerged that something very odd had been going on with the surface records on which this new claim was based: the data for the two El Niño years 1998 and 2010 had been significantly altered. The previous version of HadCRUt, known as HadCRUt 3, had shown 1998 as 0.07°C warmer than 2010. But a new HadCRUt 4 version was now showing that its figure for 1998 had been adjusted downwards and that for 2010 upwards, to give completely the opposite impression.[80]

In fact, this new claim that 2014 was now even warmer still than 1998 had been particularly based on even more dramatic new figures from GISS. This prompted an expert UK-based blogger, Paul Homewood, to investigate one of the areas of the globe where GISS was showing temperatures to have risen faster than almost anywhere else: a huge chunk of South America stretching from Brazil to Paraguay. When Homewood looked at a very large area of Paraguay that was covered by only three rural weather stations, he was startled by what he found. In each case GISS was now reporting that, between 1950 and 2014, there had been a steep temperature rise of 1.5°C: more than twice the accepted global increase for the whole of the 20th century. But the archived data giving the temperatures originally recorded during those decades had not just shown no rise: they had shown a cooling trend, amounting to a full degree!

The way this had been done became only too clear. In each case, temperatures given for the earlier years had been retrospectively 'adjusted' downwards from those originally recorded, while more recent temperatures had been 'adjusted' upwards. Thus had the picture given by the original data been turned upside down. Yet these new figures had now been fed into the global temperature record most often relied on by scientists and politicians the world over. Homewood therefore widened his search to a much larger area of South America. Again he found that similar two-way adjustments had been made, to create the impression of a warming trend not present in the original recorded data. He then turned his attention to the data for all the weather stations round a stretch of the Arctic Circle between 52°W in Canada and 87°E in Siberia (this was the part of the Arctic most affected by the recent influx of warmer water from the Atlantic). Again, in every instance, GISS had adjusted the older data downwards and that for more recent years upwards, by as much as 1°C or more.[81]

In fact, Homewood was far from alone in making such discoveries. Similar findings were being made by diligent researchers across the world, from Russia, Iceland and Ireland to South Africa, Australia and New Zealand. Almost everywhere, it seemed, the pattern was the same: older temperatures were being cooled, more recent values raised. Examination of data from specific weather stations in Australia revealed that an 80-year cooling trend equating to 1°C per century had been transformed into a warming trend of 2.3°C. In New Zealand, a considerable public row had broken out when 'unadjusted' data showing no trend up or down between 1850 and 1998 had now been 'adjusted' to give a warming trend of 0.9°C per century.[82]

And of course, all this only echoed on a much wider scale the similar findings reported by

McIntyre on *Climate Audit* in 2007, when he found that GISS had been playing the same game with the US Historical Climatology Network data. By downgrading the original recorded figures for the US in the 'dustbowl' years of the 1930s and increasing those for recent years, Hansen and Schmidt had been able to show 1998 replacing 1934 as the hottest year in American history.[83]

So serious were the implications of all these discoveries, that it might have been thought that they would provoke widespread concern, particularly when GISS and NOAA were asked to explain the reason for these systematic 'adjustments' and no convincing answer was forthcoming. But for those within the 'consensus' bubble, including scientists, politicians and the media, it seemed it was best that these startling revelations should simply be ignored.[84]

As the Paris conference approached, no politician was keener for it to succeed than the US president, Barack Obama. From the time of his first presidential campaign in 2008, he had always shown himself to be a wholly committed supporter of the 'consensus' on global warming. In his first important address after being elected, he had promised that, after years of lagging behind, America would now 'lead the world' in the fight against climate change. 'The science' he said, 'is beyond dispute'. 'Sea levels are rising, coastlines are shrinking, we've seen record drought, spreading famine, and storms that are growing stronger with each hurricane season'.

Obama promised that he would introduce a tax on 'carbon' and a cap and trade scheme, allowing businesses only to continue emitting carbon dioxide if they paid for 'carbon credits' permitting them to do so. He would spend $15 billion on building tens of thousands of new wind turbines, creating 'five million new green jobs'. The irony was that, at the very time he said all this, it was becoming clear that America had launched on a spectacular energy revolution, thanks to fracking for oil and gas buried in vast shale deposits. In just a few years, this would not only slash US gas prices by more than a half, but also make America the world's leading exporter of oil and gas.

America under Obama had thus been caught out facing both ways, with a President claiming that he wanted to follow Britain's lead in aiming to cut carbon dioxide emissions by 80 percent by 2050, while at the same time his country was benefiting from an energy bonanza like nothing the world had ever seen, based on the very fossil fuels he wanted to see eliminated.

When companies looked to repeat this astonishing success story, by fracking the extensive shale reserves in Britain and parts of Europe, they ran into a concerted and well-funded campaign of opposition, painting the technology as a complete environmental disaster, polluting groundwater, setting off earthquakes and even causing water from kitchen taps to catch fire. So influential was this largely unopposed campaign that the public, certainly in Britain where the BBC in particular eagerly joined in, was left almost wholly unaware that these claims were no more than almost wholly fictitious propaganda. For a long time, it looked like yet another victory for organised groupthink. And even when, in 2016, the British government was at last to give the go-ahead to a limited amount of tightly-regulated fracking, the initiative seemed doomed in due course to run into Britain's legal commitment to phase out virtually all fossil fuels.

Despite Britain being given a possible chance to secure her energy future for generations to come, there seemed little prospect that she would enjoy anything like the success of America, even though to its President this was an embarrassment he was anxious never to mention. Similarly, nothing more was heard of his promised five million new 'green' jobs.

18 Paris 2015: a final 'triumph' for groupthink

> Today is a historic day in the fight to protect our planet for future generations. This gives us the best possible shot to save the one planet we got.[sic]
>
> President Obama [85]

> This is the first time in the history of mankind that we are setting ourselves the task of intentionally, within a defined period of time, to change the economic development model that has been reigning for at least 150 years, since the industrial revolution.
>
> Christiana Figueres, chief UNFCCC organiser of the Paris conference, Brussels, February 2015

One reason why those within the bubble had been so eager to proclaim 2014 as the 'hottest year on record' was their need to whip up expectations for the great Paris climate conference in December 2015. The general aim was that, after the failure in Copenhagen to agree a successor to the Kyoto Protocol, the nations of the world must this time really succeed in signing a legally binding treaty committing them all to a massive reduction in emissions of carbon dioxide and a wholesale shift away from fossil fuels. Every stop had to be pulled out. For President Obama, due to step down in 2017, it was to be his crowning 'legacy'. Even the Pope was wheeled on, to sign a papal encyclical calling for drastic action on reducing the use of fossil fuels for the sake of the world's poor.[86]

The target was to prevent global temperatures from rising any more than 2°C above where they had been, as the 'consensus' argued, before the industrial revolution set the world on its catastrophic course (or, as others had it, the world began naturally to warm again as it emerged from the Little Ice Age). And as the date for them all to gather in Paris drew nearer, the clamour grew for even that 2°C target to be lowered to just 1.5°C.

The general principle underlying the proposed treaty was that first put forward by Maurice Strong at Rio in 1992 and again at Kyoto and Copenhagen. The nations of the world would be divided into two categories. The first, the developed Western countries, would all agree to making drastic emissions cuts, and they would also pay $100 billion a year into a new 'Green Climate Fund', to assist those countries in the second category, the rest of the world, in following suit by doing their best to curb their own use of fossil fuels.

In the months before the conference, every country was asked by the UNFCCC to submit what was called an Intended Nationally Determined Contribution (INDC). This was to be its own 'Climate Action Plan', setting out in detail just how it proposed to meet the aims of the proposed treaty in the years up to 2030. At first sight, almost all of these opaquely written national submissions gave the desired impression, namely that they were only too keen to co-operate with the 'decarbonisation' agenda. Those from the 'developing' countries made much mention of their 'renewables' targets, and their proposed efforts to reduce carbon dioxide emissions, although they did expect to be generously rewarded for this from the 'Green Climate Fund', funded by the developed countries.

But when careful examination came to be given to each of the INDCs submitted by the 20 countries that were the world's heaviest emitters of carbon dioxide, responsible between them for 81 percent of all global emissions, a very different picture emerged. And it was one entirely missed by the world's media.[87]

Buried away in the figures submitted by China, now easily the world's largest single emitter, contributing 24 percent of the global total, it emerged that it was actually planning by 2030 to double its carbon dioxide emissions, not least by building hundreds more coal-fired power stations.

The INDC submitted by India, by now the world's third largest emitter, showed that it too was planning to build even more coal-fired power stations, which by 2030 would contribute to a trebling of its annual emissions.

The fourth largest emitter, Russia, despite having slashed its emissions after 1990 by closing down many of the old Soviet industries, was now proposing to increase them from their 2012 level by up to 38 percent. Japan, which was the fifth largest emitter, claimed that it hoped to cut its emissions by some 15 percent, but was still planning to build more coal-fired power plants.

Although South Korea, seventh on the emissions list, claimed that it would be cutting emissions by 23 percent (not least by buying 'carbon credits' which would allow them to 'offset' their continuing production of carbon dioxide), even its proposed target would still be 100 percent higher than it had been in 1990.

By the deadline, the Middle Eastern oil states, Saudi Arabia and Iran, the eighth and ninth largest emitters, had not even submitted their proposals. But the United Arab Emirates, which had more than doubled their emissions since 2002, gave no indication of any plans to slow that increase, apart from a promise to invest in more 'carbon free' solar and nuclear power.

As for Brazil, the eleventh largest emitter, which had been rapidly increasing its dependence on fossil fuels, it now offered as its main contribution that it would take steps to slow down the clearing and burning of the Amazon rainforest.

But what about the countries most obviously missing from this list? President Obama may have repeatedly talked the talk about his ambitious plans for the US, as the world's second largest emitter after China, but there was no more chance of Congress agreeing to the proposed treaty than there had been in 1997 when the Senate unanimously voted 'no' to Kyoto. All of which left, as the only part of the world already committed to cutting its emissions by 40 percent by 2030, the European Union. But even here, Poland was already refusing to sign the treaty, as it continued to build more fossil-fuel power stations to keep its lights on. Germany, the world's sixth largest emitter, despite having built 26,000 wind turbines and pouring billions of euros into solar power, was planning to do the same.

The only government in the world wholly committed to meeting that 40 percent target by 2030 under its Climate Change Act was that of the UK, the 14th largest emitter, by now responsible for only 1.3 percent of the global total. This was less than China or India were each now adding every year, as Britain continued to shut down those fossil-fuel power plants that in 2015 still provided two-thirds of its electricity.

As for the Green Climate Fund, which it was hoped would, by 2020, be handing out $100 billion each year to help developing countries 'adapt to climate change', it emerged, as the Paris conference approached, that firm pledges so far received from the developed nations amounted to just $700 million. This left $99.3 billion still to be found, just to pay for the fund's first year.[88]

At the start of December 40,000 politicians, officials, green activists, lobbyists and journalists from 195 nations converged on a huge, specially-built venue outside Paris, appropriately at an airport largely reserved for private jets.

The outcome, as before, was entirely predictable. After two weeks of fractious behind-the-scenes haggling, the weary-looking dignitaries assembled on the platform of the main conference hall to put as brave a face on the result as they could, as they congratulated each other on having reached a 'historic agreement'. This was what they and the media were to tell the world. But the truth was that almost the only item on the agenda on which everyone had been persuaded to agree was that each nation would submit a further statement of its progress and intentions every five years. Despite every attempt made to pretend otherwise, there was no legally binding treaty. As I wrote the following Sunday, below a picture of the Eiffel Tower emblazoned with the huge illuminated slogan '1.5°C':

> No sooner last weekend were world leaders congratulating themselves on having reached their 'historic agreement' to save the planet by scrapping all those 'dirty' fossil-fuels than two groups normally bitterly opposed to each other were united in deriding the meaningless absurdity of what had happened.
>
> The ultra-greens, led by the 'father of the global warming scare' James Hansen, immediately hailed an agreement which committed no-one to anything as no more than a 'fake' and a 'fraud'. Clued-up climate sceptics equally recognised that this much-vaunted 'non-treaty' was indeed – precisely as I predicted here on November 1 – 'the flop of the year'.
>
> It really is time for us all to grasp just what a charade all that wishful thinking in Paris turned out to be. Lost in their self-deluding groupthink, the 40,000 delegates may have been happy to cheer the idea that we must abolish fossil fuels. But not one pointed out that the world currently depends on fossil fuels to provide nearly 82 percent of all the energy it uses. Those useless 'renewables' they want us all to use instead – based on the wind and the sun – supply less than 2 percent.
>
> But equally buried from sight in Paris was the openly declared intention of China, India and pretty well every 'emerging economy' in the world to build thousands more coal-fired power stations, causing their 'carbon emissions' to double or even treble. Global emissions in the next 15 years are set to soar, without any effect on the climate whatever. All of which leaves the countries of the West, which fooled the media into thinking that anything at all had been achieved by that PR stunt in Paris, in a ludicrously isolated position. And none more so than Britain. now the only country in the world legally committed, by the Climate Change Act, to reduce its carbon dioxide emissions by 80 percent within 35 years.[89]

The pretence that Paris had resulted in a 'legally binding treaty' was to continue for months to come, faithfully reported by the media, with little sign of any attempt to look at the facts of what had really happened.

The one thing which more than any was temporarily to save the face of the 'consensus' cause over the following year was the unpredicted arrival of a record-breaking El Niño, which by 2016 had pushed global temperatures so high that even the two satellite records reported that 2016 tied for warmth with 1998.

Although this was a natural event, the temperature spike in 2015 and 2016 had equally naturally been greeted as proof that at last the embarrassing 'pause' had ended, and that the rise in man-made global warming was back on track. But even before 2016 was over, the satellites were again showing a dramatic collapse in temperatures. By the end of 2016 it was no longer standing out as 'the hottest year ever' and by the middle of 2017 the fall in temperatures had amounted to more than 0.6°C. Once again, those predictions by groupthink-inspired computer models that temperatures would rise through the 21st century by an average of 0.3°C or more per decade had been proved wrong. The 'pause' was back.

At this point we can break off from this chronological summary of the global warming story, the purpose of which has been to show how at every stage this had been governed by the three defining rules of groupthink.

Naturally this has left out countless other relevant examples. But this paper would not be complete without reference to one more example, the consequences and implications of which are so immense that it can be properly regarded as 'the other half' of the entire story. I discuss this in two parts: firstly the general picture and then the specific and in some ways unique example of the United Kingdom.

19 The real global warming disaster: how groupthink shaped the political response

> Future generations will wonder in bemused amazement that the early 21st century's developed world went into hysterical panic over a globally averaged temperature increase of a few tenths of a degree and, on the basis of gross exaggerations of highly uncertain computer projections combined into implausible of inference, proceeded to contemplate a roll-back of the industrial age.
>
> Dr Richard Lindzen

By far the most extraordinary achievement of the panic over 'man-made global warming' was the way it managed to demonise carbon dioxide, a trace gas vital to all life on earth, as a dangerous 'pollutant'. Equally demonised, therefore, were those sources of energy based on fossil fuels, coal, gas and oil, on which all modern industrial civilisation had been built. Wherever possible, according to the groupthink, these had to be described as 'dirty' (as opposed to the 'clean' energy from renewables), and had to be phased out or eliminated from human activity.

As I suggested in the title of my book *The Real Global Warming Disaster*, 'man-made climate change' was indeed heading the world towards a catastrophe. But this was not the one conjured up by the 'true believers': soaring temperatures, vanishing ice caps, flooded cities, 'extreme weather', 'climate chaos', 'mass-extinctions', even a threat to the survival of life on earth. None of this was happening in the way they liked to claim. The real disaster now threatening lay in the measures being adopted in consequence of that panic, based on the belief that the only way to 'save the planet' was to 'decarbonise' the world's economies. And this was to be done by the wholesale abandonment of those 'polluting' fossil fuels, which by 2014, according to the International Energy Agency, were still supplying more than four-fifths of all the energy the world was using.[90] Instead, of course, the groupthink dictated that we must move as fast as possible to relying on those sources of energy which supposedly did not emit carbon dioxide. This would amount to a complete revolution in how the energy to power the global economy was produced. The line was that in future it should be centred on 'renewables' and on a massive expansion of nuclear power.

Indeed, scores of nations were now moving to adopt such a policy, most notably the US under President Obama and the countries of the European Union, but this drive to 'decarbonise' brought with it two massive problems, which those promoting it invariably did all they could to hide, deny or obfuscate by playing implausible tricks with the figures.

One was simply the cost. Nowhere in the world had it proved possible to switch to 'zero carbon' energy sources without the aid of colossal subsidies. The actual cost of 'renewable' and even nuclear power was up to four or even more times higher than that derived from coal.

The second huge problem was that the two 'renewable' technologies that had attracted most attention, wind and solar, were so unreliable because of the inescapable fact that they were wholly dependent on the vagaries of the weather. There was nothing their advocates were more reluctant to admit than that wind turbines and solar panels could only produce electricity irregularly, unpredictably and therefore at only a fraction of their potential capacity. In the case of wind turbines this averaged out at a third or less of their optimum power; for solar panels, except in parts of the world where the sun could be relied on to shine most of the time, it averaged out, as in northern Europe, at only around 10 percent.[91]

But the more of these wind and solar farms that got built, the more the constant fluctuation of their output created serious technical problems for electricity grids. To keep supply and demand in balance, they needed instantly available back-up. And this could not be provided by coal or nuclear power, which were designed to generate 'baseload' electricity, and could not suddenly increase their output to meet a sharp rise in demand,

The only energy source flexible enough to provide that instantly available back-up when needed was natural gas, which unlike the others could be quickly ramped up and down. In other words, the only way to keep a grid balanced was by means of one of those 'polluting' fossil-fuels the groupthinkers wished to see the back of.

The astonishing fact was that, by 2015, despite more than $1 trillion having been poured into building hundreds of thousands of wind turbines and solar farms across the world, the amount of the world's energy needs they supplied was still almost infinitesimally small. In 2014, according to the IEA's *2016 Key Renewables Trends*, wind contributed only 0.46 percent of total global energy; solar and tidal power just 0.35 percent. These thus amounted between them to less than 1 percent.[92] Yet so carried away by make-believe were politicians and the media that hardly anywhere outside technical reports were these figures reported.

And despite the lip-service that so many countries were now paying to the need for more 'renewables', those national submissions by every country before the Paris conference showed that most of the 'developing' countries were still between them planning to build huge numbers of coal-fired power stations to keep their economies growing. From their own figures, it was possible to calculate that this would result by 2030 in a rise of 46 percent in carbon dioxide emissions in just 15 years.

20 The peculiar case of the United Kingdom

> We will continue to take a lead in global action against climate change, as the government demonstrated by ratifying the Paris Agreement. We were the first country to introduce a Climate Change Act.
>
> Conservative Party election manifesto, 2017

In no country in the world were the contradictions of this make-believe policy more evident than in Britain, the only nation committed by law to reduce carbon dioxide emissions by more than 80 percent.[93] Thus was the government planning to phase out almost all use of the fossil-fuels which, in 2015, were still providing 82 percent of all the country's energy. There was no better illustration of the illusory world this had carried the politicians into than a document first published by the Department for Energy and Climate Change in 2011, entitled *2050 Pathways*. After 2030, for instance, almost wholly unnoticed by the media, this envisaged an end to all use of gas for cooking and heating, on which 90 percent of households relied, to be replaced instead by electricity. The transport system would likewise come to be largely reliant on electricity, including, by 2030, 60 percent of all cars.

All this and more, DECC proposed, would require a doubling of Britain's electricity supply, to be provided almost entirely by a massive expansion of 'renewables', such as offshore windfarms, and a new fleet of nuclear reactors. New fossil-fuel power stations might still be permitted, but only on condition that they were fitted with 'carbon capture and storage', to pipe away their carbon dioxide emissions into holes under the North Sea (using a technology not even yet developed).

If this seemed to be pure *Alice in Wonderland* fantasy (on the lines of the White Queen recalling how she managed to 'believe as many as six impossible things before breakfast'), by 2017 it could be measured against the reality of what had happened to all the bewildering array of 'green' schemes the government had already put its hand to.

Making national headlines in March 2017 was 'Diesel-gate', reporting that particulates emitted from diesel-powered vehicles were now such a problem that they were allegedly causing anything between 12,000 and 40,000 premature deaths a year. But the wholesale switch to diesel, which had now put 14 million such vehicles on Britain's roads, had been engineered through the tax system, on the advice in 2001 of Sir David King, when he was the government's chief scientific adviser, after he was told that diesel emitted a smaller amount of planet-warming carbon dioxide than petrol.

In Northern Ireland in January 2017, the coalition government collapsed, creating its worst political crisis since the end of the Troubles. This came about through a major scandal over a government 'green' scheme, the Renewable Heat Incentive, under which businesses had been offered almost unlimited subsidies to heat their premises with wood chip boilers. So many had rushed to claim £160 in subsidy for every £100 they paid for wood chips that they were running their boilers round the clock, even to heat factories, offices and warehouses no longer in use. The total subsidy bill, it had now been estimated, would by 2020 have soared to £1 billion.

A similar, little-noticed racket was already going on in England: under the same scheme, owners of large houses openly boasted to friends that they were able to keep their wood-chip heating systems going full-blast even at the height of summer, because they were making a 60 percent profit on all the fuel they burned (which contributed to the fact that Britain was now said to be burning more wood than at any time since the Napoleonic wars).

Another example, which did hit the headlines in March 2017, was Drax in Yorkshire, once the largest, cleanest, most efficient coal-fired power station in Europe. Under a different 'green' subsidy scheme, it was now converting its boilers to burning 'biomass': millions of tons of wood pellets a year, shipped 3800 miles across the Atlantic from the forests of North Carolina.

It paid Drax to do this because a swingeing government 'carbon tax' had deliberately made it increasingly unprofitable to burn coal. On the other hand, for burning wood (officially rated by the EU as 'carbon neutral', because eventually new trees would supposedly absorb the carbon dioxide emitted by burning the wood pellets), Drax was now receiving a subsidy of £500 million a year. But a report from Chatham House had confirmed that Drax was now emitting more carbon dioxide per unit of electricity than it did when only burning coal.

Another scandal just coming to light was the way developers were now receiving more than £200 million a year in subsidies, again under the Renewable Heat Incentive, for erecting large industrial 'anaerobic digesters' in the countryside, to turn huge quantities of farm crops into methane for the national gas grid. No less than 131,000 acres of maize alone were now being grown for this purpose, on land formerly used to produce food. But this was now arousing serious environmental concern over spills of highly toxic ammonia used in the process, which had killed livestock and fish in fields and rivers.

At least the government was still havering over a £40 billion project, formerly supported by prime minister David Cameron, to build six gigantic tidal power station round Britain's coasts. For such a colossal outlay, these would only produce relatively small amounts of some of the most expensive electricity in the world, while they would also, conservationists warned, cause serious environmental damage to wading birds, fish including migratory eels, and other wildlife.

But by far the greatest environmental damage, at the greatest cost to electricity users, had been done through the £100 billion spent on covering vast areas of Britain's land and sea with 7500-plus wind turbines and solar farms. These were already costing £4.6 billion a year in subsidies, and the bill was now rising so fast that by 2022, according to the Office for Budget Responsibility (OBR), they would add up to a further £31 billion.[94]

Even though by now these 'renewables' were producing 14 percent of Britain's electricity, the actual output was so unpredictable that, if it hadn't been for the remaining carbon dioxide-emitting gas-fired power stations ready to step in when the wind wasn't blowing, Britain might already have been experiencing major power cuts.

But the biggest headlines of all, in July 2017, were reserved for the government's announcement that, from 2040 onwards, it would become illegal in Britain to make, import or sell any cars powered by petrol or diesel. All new cars from that date on would have to be all-electric. Successive governments had been pushing motorists to switch to electric cars for several years, allocating £400 million of taxpayers' money in subsidies to bribe them to do so. Despite this, there were many practical reasons why these had not caught on, and they so far comprised only 0.3 percent of the 31.7 million cars on Britain's roads.

But the most crucial question raised by this plan to ban any but all-electric cars by 2040 was where was all the extra electricity needed to power them to come from? This, it was estimated, could be as much as 30 gigawatts (GW). This alone would add nearly 50 percent to Britain's current peak electricity demand of 61 GW, more than half of it still supplied by the fossil fuels the Government wished to see eliminated.

The government's answer was that it would come from wind and nuclear power. But to produce another 30 GW from wind turbines alone would require an additional 100 GW of capacity, bringing the number of new turbines needed to 30–40,000, five times more than the 7,600 already installed. And, on windless or near-windless days and nights, these would not charge the batteries of many electric cars.

As for nuclear, to produce 30 GW would require some nine more new nuclear power stations the size of the only one the government had already committed itself to, planned at Hinkley Point, at a capital cost of £24 billion (with a lifetime cost including subsidies of £50 billion). But this itself was unlikely to be completed (if it ever is) before 2030, and no more were yet firmly in the pipeline.

Even before this latest scheme had to be factored in, the costs of the government's existing 'decarbonisation' policy were soaring to astronomic levels. Projections by the OBR in March 2017 showed that by 2022 the annual cost of all 'green' taxes and subsides was due to rise from £8.97 billion a year to £15.2 billion. This would by 2022 bring the five-year total to £73 billion, a figure far higher than the estimated cost of the projected HS2 rail scheme, which is the most expensive engineering project ever seen in Britain. The cost equated by 2022 to £584 a year for every household in the land.

Not for nothing had prime minister Theresa May's then-joint-chief of staff, Nick Timothy, described the Climate Change Act in April 2016 as 'a unilateral and monstrous act of national self-harm'. But at the 2017 general election the Conservative Party manifesto made no fewer than three mentions of how Britain was now 'leading the world in taking action against climate change'. It even made that boast, quoted above, that Britain had been the first country in the world 'to introduce a Climate Change Act'.

No other country, of course, had followed the British example. China and India alone were each adding more new carbon dioxide to the atmosphere each year than Britain's entire annual emissions, which now amounted to only 1.1 percent of the global total.

In this respect, those running Britain – not to mention pretty well all those who held sway over public opinion, such as the media – were still so blinded by the all-prevailing groupthink that it could not allow any chink of reality to break in.

21 President Trump finally calls the groupthink's bluff

> Under the agreement, China will be able to increase these emissions for a staggering number of years...Not us....China will be allowed to build hundreds of additional coal plants...we can't build the plants, but they can, according to this agreement...India can double their coal production. We're supposed to get rid of ours. In short...this agreement is less about the climate and more about other countries gaining a financial advantage over the United States. The rest of the world applauded when we signed the Paris agreement – they went wild; they were so happy – for the simple reason that it put our country...at a very, very big economic disadvantage.
>
> President Trump, 1 June 2017

> Rest of world rallies around Paris deal.
>
> BBC News website, 2 June 2017

> President Trump can turn his back on the world, but the world cannot ignore the very real threat of climate change. This decision is an immoral assault on the public health, safety and security of everyone on this planet.
>
> Bill de Blasio, Mayor of New York, 1 June 2017

There could have been no more appropriate event on which to end this narrative than the near-universal howl of disbelief and rage that greeted President Trump's announcement in the Rose Garden of the White House on 1 June 2017 that he was pulling the US out of the Paris 'climate accord'. World leaders and other senior politicians immediately joined with much of the media in expressing utter shock and dismay at what the Democrat leader in the Senate called 'one of the worst policy moves made in the 21st century'. Trump had scarcely finished speaking before the BBC had wheeled on someone to describe his decision as 'apocalyptic, paranoid and delusional'. Social media went into near-meltdown, with screaming abuse and messages of which one of the mildest was 'climate deniers are in for a very rude awakening when u can no longer breathe clean air, and your kids are sick from pollution'.

But the most remarkable feature of Trump's speech, which they all missed, was how he stripped away the spin and misrepresentation which back in December 2015 had led even that celebrated climate zealot James Hansen to scorn the Paris Agreement as no more than a 'fake' and a 'fraud'. Trump pointed out that, contrary to all the attempts made to pretend otherwise, Paris was not a 'legally binding treaty'. But even more important, he was also the first politician to expose what had been the real dirty secret of Paris, buried away in those INDCs, setting out how, by 2030, each country intended to respond to the proposed 'climate goals'. Herein lay the central fraud of the entire agreement. The 'developing' countries, led by China and India, certainly had their eye on that proposed Green Climate Fund, whereby the developed countries would supposedly pay them $100 billion every year to assist them to 'decarbonise', above all by going for 'renewables'. The developing countries had all thus paid lip-service up-front to what was required, and how they planned to expand their 'renewable' energy sources: wind, solar and the rest. But hidden in the small print, as Trump highlighted, was the real story. China and India, as the first and third largest carbon dioxide emitting countries in the world, were each planning to build hundreds of new coal-fired power stations, which alone would by 2030 double and treble their emissions. Analysis of the INDCs showed that almost every one of the larger developing nations planned something not dissimilar. As for that Green Climate Fund, as Trump went on to explain, it was also just make-believe. By now, only $1 billion had been pledged, of which almost all, thanks to Obama, had been offered by the US.

Trump's speech may have been justifiably America-centric, in talking of how the US had been committed by Obama to paying by far the highest economic price in terms of money and lost jobs, for a deal whereby China, India and the rest would take America's money but carry on emitting carbon dioxide just as before. This was why the President was entirely justified in pulling the US out of a non-binding deal as fraudulent as any major international agreement can ever have been. But just as significant was that none of those now accusing him of 'betraying the future of the planet' appeared to be even remotely aware of any of the facts he had been addressing. So lost were they in their bubble that their only response was either just to resort to hysterical abuse or, by some, to claim that Trump's decision would make little difference to the battle to save the planet. This was because the EU and everyone else would be united in complying with the 'Accord', while China would now 'take the lead' in renewables and the great 'low carbon' revolution.

All this was as perfect an example of the power of groupthink as could be imagined. President Trump, like no politician before him, had finally called the bluff of the make-believe. But so firmly cocooned from reality were the politicians and the media that none of them had even begun to realise it.

22 Conclusions: what happens when the groupthink does meet reality?

> The precise moment at which a great belief is doomed is easily recognisable: it is the moment when its value is called in question. Every general belief being no more than a fiction, it can only survive on the condition that it be not subjected to examination.
>
> Gustave Le Bon, *The Crowd*

The conclusions of this paper are divided into three parts. The first gives a general retrospective overview on what was the fatal flaw in the groupthink that drove the global warming scare. The second summarises some of the more obvious reasons why the groupthink has become so powerfully entrenched that it might be hard to imagine how its grip could be broken. But the third suggests that in practice this is already happening. Recent events have confirmed that the supposed worldwide political 'consensus' that man-made global warming poses an unprecedented threat to the future of the planet has never been a true consensus at all. And this has finally begun to change the entire story.

Groupthink's fatal flaw

'Nullius in verba': The motto of the Royal Society

Future generations may look back on the late-20th and early 21st-century panic over man-made warming as one of the strangest episodes in the history of either science or politics. But they will only be able to understand how such an extraordinary flight from reality could have taken place by reference to the peculiarities of collective human psychology, and in particular to the rules defining the nature of groupthink. Of course, the world had seen such triumphs of groupthink before, as in the history of its great religions or the way the belief-system based on Marxism held sway across such a vast area of the world through much of the 20th century.

In crucial respects the ideology of global warming has much in common with these examples. Like them, it originated with only a very small group of people, who had become gripped by a visionary idea. Like them, it was based on predictions of a hypothetical future – or prophecies – which could not be definitively proved right or wrong. Like them it therefore became important to insist that this belief-system must be subscribed to by a 'consensus' of all right-thinking people, and using every kind of social, political and psychological pressure to enforce conformity with it. And like them this inevitably shaped the response to anyone who would not be a part of it, who therefore had to be condemned as a 'heretic', a 'subversive' or a 'denier', and whose dissent had to be more or less ruthlessly suppressed.

What made this latest example different from the others, however, was that it was based on the unrivalled authority accorded in the modern world to science.[95] And herein lay what would eventually prove to be its fatal weakness. Unlike those other belief-systems, it could ultimately be tested against empirically verifiable facts. It crucially rested on those all-important computer model predictions which, as the years went by, could increasingly be compared with the objective evidence of what was actually happening.

For its first 10 years or so, as we know, the theory that the world was warming as a direct result of the rise in atmospheric carbon dioxide still seemed plausible. But increasingly after 1998 the predictions and the real-world evidence began to diverge. And the response of those within the groupthink was not, as the principles of proper science should have dictated, to ask whether the theory itself might therefore be in some way flawed.

Some scientists from within the 'consensus' did indeed try to come up with modifications to the theory that might explain why the predictions were no longer being confirmed by the evidence. Around 2007, with a startling drop in global temperatures, they for the first time began to wonder whether 'natural factors', such as shifts in the world's major ocean currents might not be having more influence on shaping the climate than the IPCC's computer models had allowed for.[96] Eventually even the IPCC and the UK Met Office acknowledged that there had been a temperature 'pause' in the years after 1998. But they too tried to explain this away by suggesting that these natural factors were merely 'masking the underlying warming trend', which in due course would re-emerge. Or they suggested that the heat created by man-made warming was only no longer visible because it was 'hiding in the oceans'.

This claim was supported by the IPCC's Fifth Assessment Report in 2013, which accepted that '93 percent' of the extra heat entering the world during the pause had been absorbed by the oceans, with only 1 percent of it raising temperatures at the earth's land surface.[97] Other scientists simply ignored the growing evidence that the models had got it wrong, or worse still started to manipulate the evidence, as in all that wholesale 'adjustment' of the surface temperature records, to show that the world was indeed still warming as the theory had predicted. Indeed, nothing should have aroused clearer suspicion that something was fundamentally questionable about the theory than the repeated attempts by those within the 'consensus' to manipulate the scientific data to support their case. The supreme example of this, of course, had been all those tortuous efforts to 'get rid of the Medieval Warm Period' and show that the world was now hotter than at any time in history.

What is also highly relevant to our understanding of how this all came about, however, was the remarkable readiness, not just of the scientific community itself, but also of politicians, the media and so many others, to accept the man-made warming thesis without ever questioning it.

At the beginning of this paper, in a section headed 'the power of second-hand thinking', we looked at the obvious way in which the vast majority of people who went along with the 'consensus' only did so because they had never given it any serious study or examined the evidence themselves. They had simply taken their opinions from what they had been told by others. In this sense, acceptance of the 'consensus' mindset was like a contagious condition. Any attempt to question those who had passed under its spell as to why they believed what they did all too often revealed that they didn't really know anything about it at all. Their heads were filled with a ragbag of mantras and gobbets of misinformation (such as that the vanishing of Arctic ice was threatening the survival of polar bears), which were so often demonstrably the very reverse of the truth.

And this was not just true of many members of the general public. It was equally true of people paid or qualified to know better, such as environmental journalists, politicians, indeed a great many scientists themselves. A neighbour of mine was a reputable professor of chemistry at a leading university and, when he spoke about global warming, he liked to claim that he did so with the authority of 'a scientist'. But he would then solemnly tell us that the rise in sea levels caused by climate change would eventually submerge our village, even though it was several hundred feet up on the hills of Somerset.

It is this blur of firmly convinced ignorance that reveals one of the more conspicuous characteristics of the 'true believers': that it is impossible for those outside the 'consensus' ever to have any serious dialogue with them. Those possessed by groupthink were convinced that they just 'knew' what it was they thought they knew. They were used to talking about it only to those who shared the same beliefs. They were incapable of focussing properly on any evidence that might seem to contradict their certainties.

It was this which too often brought into play Janis's third rule: the only response to those who disagreed with them was, first, incredulity that anyone could be so silly, and then to resort to the kind of scornful abuse they considered to be the only appropriate way to deal with these 'deniers', who could just be caricatured as no better than 'flat earthers', conspiracy theorists who could be contemptuously dismissed because they were 'anti-science'.

In reality, of course, it was the sceptics themselves, such as Richard Lindzen and Paul Reiter, who were trying to defend proper science. They also eventually included, for instance, such eminent figures in the world scientific community as the two veteran Princeton physicists, Freeman Dyson and Will Happer. It was the supporters of the 'consensus', as they could see, who had tragically betrayed the principles of proper science.

But this was equally true of those grand figures at the very top of the 'consensus' hierarchy. As we have seen, it was precisely this same attitude that was displayed by the senior scientists responsible for the Climategate emails; or by such prestigious figures as the 'chief scientist' Sir David King, or those presidents of the Royal Society, Lord May and Sir Paul Nurse. How ironic, it was observed (not least by many dissenting members of the Royal Society itself), that the defining motto of the oldest and long most respected scientific society in the world had since the 1660s, been 'nullius in verba', commonly translated as 'take nobody's word for it'. As countless distinguished members of that august society had known since the days of Robert Hooke, Robert Boyle and Isaac Newton, there is no principle of scientific method more fundamental than this. No new scientific proposition should be accepted as true solely 'on the word of others', unless they can demonstrate that it is properly supported by evidence. To test any hypothesis, one must look at *all* the evidence, making sure that any which might invalidate the theory has also been fully taken into account.

All this was what the 'carbon dioxide equals global warming' theory had turned on its head. Almost the entire Western scientific community had been so carried away by the simplicity of the theory that they never subjected it to proper three-dimensional scientific questioning. They programmed their computer models accordingly. And the only response considered necessary to an argument suggesting that the theory might in some way be flawed was just to ignore or ridicule it.

Even when ever more evidence began to suggest that the theory was not being borne out as predicted, the response was either to find ways to modify the theory round the edges, so that it could still be held onto intact, or simply to invent new 'facts' to make the theory still seem plausible. Thus, right from the start, the entire house of cards had been based on 'taking other people's word for it', without ever putting the hypothesis to the test or allowing any genuine scientific debate. Again and again, however hard they tried to torture the evidence into seeming to support their theory, those hard facts kept on intruding to suggest otherwise.

That is why, one day, future generations will eventually look back at this story in disbelieving astonishment: to ask 'how on earth could such a thing have happened?'.

Before we move on to the second of our conclusions, it is not inappropriate to quote those words attributed to Isaac Newton:

> I seem to have been only like a boy playing on the sea shore, and diverting myself in now and then finding a smoother pebble or a prettier shell than ordinary, while the great ocean of truth lay all undiscovered before me.

...and then to add a word on the relevance to the 'consensus' on global warming of that seminal book by Thomas S. Kuhn, *The Structure of Scientific Revolutions* (1962). Kuhn's thesis was that the history of science has been characterised by the prevalence of ruling 'paradigms', which provide an overall consensus in some area of science within which the vast majority of scientists continue to think and work so long as their particular paradigm continues to be generally accepted. One of the most famous examples discussed by Kuhn was the Aristotelian/Ptolemaic geocentric cosmology, which had held sway for more than 1500 years. This paradigm only finally began to give way when Copernicus developed his new cosmological model, finally published just before his death in 1543, placing the Sun at the centre of the solar system. But even then, it took a long time for the Copernican model to win full acceptance, because the hold of the old geocentric paradigm continued to remain so powerful (as Galileo found to his cost nearly a century later).

Another familiar example of a rather speedier paradigm shift, not mentioned by Kuhn, was that which followed Louis Pasteur's challenge to the ruling orthodoxy that one of the major causes of diseases was their 'spontaneous generation' in 'foul air' (the so-called 'miasma' theory). Pasteur was able to show that the real cause of these diseases, and much else, was the presence in the air of the micro-organisms later more specifically differentiated as bacteria and viruses. But even Pasteur initially ran into bitter opposition from those locked into the existing paradigm, because it was on this that all their thinking, careers and reputations relied. They could not think outside their familiar bubble.

We are confronted today with a similar problem over the consensus on global warming, which has established itself as the ruling paradigm of our time, centred on that simple equation between greenhouse gases and temperatures.

Kuhn showed how – long before a paradigm finally comes to be superseded – awkward 'anomalies' often come to light, which those within it try to explain without abandoning their belief in the established consensus. This, of course, is what has happened with the 'rising carbon dioxide equals rising temperatures' orthodoxy. All sorts of anomalies have arisen, from the failure of the computer models to predict observed evidence, to all those natural factors influencing climate that the paradigm is too crude to take proper account: shifts in the major ocean currents, solar radiation, and the implausibility of the needed positive feedback effect of water vapour, without which large warming is impossible.

As Kuhn observed, a real paradigm shift can only take place when a new theory emerges which accounts for all the evidence more plausibly than that which it has replaced. And the trouble with the over-simple global warming theory is that, despite enough anomalies having arisen to suggest that it is wholly inadequate to explain all the evidence, no new theory has yet emerged comprehensive enough to replace it.

And the reason for this is frustratingly simple. We have now learned enough to know that what really shapes the climate is far more complex than any one theoretical framework can yet hope to accommodate. We have many new pieces of the jigsaw but not yet the complete picture they represent.

We have indeed begun to recognise that natural factors , for example the El Niño–Southern Oscillation, have much more influence on global temperatures than the paradigm allowed for. Something of the interactions of climate with solar radiation has been known about ever since the connection was first observed by William Herschel in 1801, and much important new work has been done on the subject in the past 30 years. But no-one has yet begun to produce a comprehensive explanation for the fluctuations in global temperatures since the Earth emerged from the last ice age (let alone what we know about those even more dramatic fluctuations stretching back through geological time before that).

What caused the rise in temperatures that produced the Medieval Warm Period? Or the fall in temperatures that led to the centuries-long Little Ice Age which followed? What then accounted for the return to rising temperatures which has marked the two centuries of the modern warming, of which the modest further temperature rise of the past 30 years can be seen as just part of a continuum?

The truth is that we simply do not have proper explanations for any of these natural events. The more we learn about all the different factors which undoubtedly play their part in shaping the world's climate, the more we have to accept that it still presents us with too many 'unknowns', both known and unknown.

But, unlike Newton, the last thing too many scientists can afford to admit is how much they don't really know. Much safer to stay within the bubble, which seems to provide an easy explanation, and to ignore or ridicule anyone suggesting that there might be 'more things in heaven and earth' than are dreamed of in their paradigm.

So where does this leave the world?: When or how will reality finally break in?

> If there is an insignificant increase in the temperature, it is not due to anthropogenic factors but to natural factors related to the planet itself and to solar activity. There is no evidence confirming a positive linkage between the level of carbon dioxide and temperature changes...when we see the biggest international adventure based on totalitarian ideology...which tries to defend itself using disinformation and falsified facts, it is hard to think of any other word to describe this but 'war'.
>
> Alexander Ilarionov, Moscow 2004[98]

The question observers familiar with this story have long been asking is this: when and how will reality at last begin to break in? What are the possible factors which might finally begin to dispel such a fog of delusion?

The real problem, of course, is that, above all in the Western world, the groupthink paradigm has become so all-pervasive that in 2017 it is still hard to imagine how its grip can eventually be broken. And the greatest obstacle to this is the extent to which so many different players in the drama have become academically, financially and ideologically dependent on it. For a start there is the spell it has come to exercise over almost the entire Western scientific establishment, including virtually all its leading scientific institutions, scientific journals and universities. With so many careers and reputations now wholly identified with the 'consensus', it is almost impossible to imagine how so many of those involved could ever change their minds. They are part of what has become known as 'the climate industry', not least the army of academics whose research funding depends on their unquestioning adherence to the official line.

Another key part of the climate industry are those 'environmental' lobby groups, such as WWF or Friends of the Earth, which have themselves become a significant part of the international climate establishment. Even now, it has still not been generally appreciated how many of these organisations receive huge sums in government funding, not just to campaign openly for the cause but also, less conspicuously, to act as pressure groups on those same governments, urging them to adopt ever more drastic measures to promote 'clean, green' energy and to eliminate 'dirty' fossil fuels.

In terms of a vested financial interest, even this pales into insignificance compared to the colossal subsidy bonanza available for all those 'green' energy schemes themselves: the hundreds of thousands of wind turbines and millions of solar panels across the world, the power stations which have switched from coal to burning 'biomass', the millions of acres of farmland switched from food to energy crops and the vast areas of rainforests cleared for 'environmentally friendly' biofuels, the latter an immense ecological disaster.

Numerous other financial interests stand firmly in the way of any backtracking on the rush to 'decarbonise', but one more must be mentioned, not just because it is so lucrative, but because it is so nakedly cynical. There is no part of the climate industry future generations may find more bizarre than the system known as 'carbon trading', originally devised under the auspices of Maurice Strong at the time of the Rio summit. [99] As has been observed, this is the modern equivalent of the late-medieval sale of 'indulgences', whereby the Papacy, in return for money, granted the gullible absolution from their sins. These days we find it hard to believe that such a delusional practice could ever have been got away with. But our own version is the system whereby, under the auspices of the UNFCCC, it has been possible to make billions from selling the right to continue emitting carbon dioxide to businesses and other organisations which, in return for buying 'carbon credits' or 'carbon offsets', can then carry on 'sinning' just as before.

With all its myriad beneficiaries, the climate industry has now swollen to such a size that, according to one study, it could now be worth worldwide as much as $1.5 trillion a year. This is greater than the entire annual GDP of all but a handful of countries.[100] And even this does not include all those countless other individuals and organisations which have become so carried away by the 'consensus' narrative that they have just unthinkingly gone along with it.[101] This is often the case even when an organisation has no possible connection with climate issues, financial or otherwise, as we saw from the way the director-general of the National Trust, one of Britain's most successful and respected charities, announced in 2015 that 'climate change' was now 'the greatest challenge' the Trust was facing. Dame Helen Ghosh, who had been the top civil servant at the Department of the Environment at the time when it was drafting the Climate Change Act, explained that the rising sea levels caused by global warming were eroding Britain's coastline, much of it owned by the Trust, by causing it to 'fall into the sea'.

Strangely, for a woman whose proper concerns were so wrapped up with preserving the nation's historic heritage, she seemed to know so little of history that she was unaware that Britain's east coast has been continually retreating and 'falling into the sea' for 6000 years, ever since rising sea levels and sinking land first made Britain an island. This added the Trust to all that army of other interest groups that have come to stand as a mighty deadweight against any rational attempt to reverse the momentum of the belief in man-made global warming, with all its horrendous political consequences.

But the groupthink driving both that belief itself and the political response to it has always essentially been centred on those countries of the Western world, which not only originated the panic over global in the first place, but have remained its main drivers ever since. Indeed, it is precisely this fact which is now turning out to be the crux of the whole story.

The West versus the rest, but without the USA

> We take note of the decision of the United States of America to withdraw from the Paris Agreement... The Leaders of the other G20 members state that the Paris Agreement is irreversible. We reiterate the importance of fulfilling the UNFCCC commitment by developed countries in providing means of implementation including financial resources to assist developing countries... We reaffirm our strong commitment to the Paris Agreement, moving swiftly towards its full implementation.
>
> Communiqué issued after G20 meeting, Hamburg, 8 July 2017

In terms of how this mighty drama will continue to unfold, by far its most significant feature is that long-familiar divide between the 'developed' countries and the rest of the world, where the power of Western groupthink has always in reality exercised very much less sway. One of the central ironies of the scare over global warming is the extent to which it became ultimately undermined by precisely that core principle that had been placed at the heart of the world's response to it by Maurice Strong, when he set up the Rio summit in 1992. This was the division of the world into two distinct groups: the Annex I nations of the West, expected to take the lead in drastically cutting their emissions, and the 'developing' countries across the rest of the world, which could be largely exempted from such restrictions until their economies had caught up with those of the West.

It was the blatantly one-sided nature of this deal which had twice-over prevented any agreement on a meaningful global 'climate treaty', in Kyoto and Copenhagen. While the Western countries embarked on ever more costly and economically damaging attempts to reduce their emissions, the economies of the 'developing' countries continued to grow, to the point where China and India had become the world's first and third largest emitters of carbon dioxide.

Then in 2015 came Paris. And if ever there was a moment when reality should finally have broken in on the West's wishful thinking, it was the publication of all those INDCs, whereby the developing nations set out how they intended to shape their energy policy for the next 15 years.

One after another, they explained how they planned to respond to what the Western world was asking for. China was intending by 2030 to raise its carbon dioxide emissions by 100 percent. India by 200 percent. Almost all the other 'developing' nations in the list of the world's top 20 emitters, along with Russia and Japan, were equally forecasting significant increases. So the overall picture that emerged was that, while the US (still under Obama) and the EU were proposing by 2030 to reduce their annual carbon dioxide emissions by 1.7 billion tonnes, India was planning to increase its emissions by 4.9 billion tonnes and China by 10.9 billion tonnes. It was certainly some deal.

The INDCs thus showed that total predicted global emissions within only 15 years would be nearly 50 percent higher than they had been in 2013.[102] This should certainly have been seen as a historically significant moment, in at least two ways. The first, obviously, was that it showed what the rest of the world thought of the West's make-believe, as its declared intentions made a total mockery of everything Paris was meant to be about. But the second point, in terms of the subject of this paper, is almost as significant. This was the extent to which the politicians and media in the West wholly failed to recognise or report what had happened. No one who learned about Paris only from the press coverage in the West would have had any idea that this was what the non-Western world was proposing. Few journalists, if any, had ever read the INDCs. What they reported was only the propagandist fluff dished out to them by the international climate establishment, as it tried to pretend that anything of genuine significance had been achieved.

This was why it came as such shock when, more than a year later, President Trump announced that he was pulling the US out of the 'Paris accord', including the Green Climate Fund. He was the first Western leader to break silence on the actual contents of those INDCs (to which he explicitly referred in his speech as delivered), showing that the 'accord' had been no more than a wholly empty sham.

At long last the West's most important politician had called into question the entire edifice of political illusions that had been so tortuously cobbled together over the previous 30 years. Whatever we may think of President Trump, or the reasons he gave for his decision, his speech finally began to undermine that ramshackle structure like nothing that had happened before.

But he was only able to do so because all those 'developing' countries had shown just what they thought of what the Western world was up to. Beyond some cynical public relations nods to the need for 'renewables', they did not give a fig for what the Western groupthink had wanted them to do or say: they would carry on with their economic growth, based on burning vast quantities of precisely those same fossil-fuels which the groupthink wanted to see eliminated from the earth.

Despite the pretences of the communiqué issued after the first G20 meeting attended by Trump in July 2017, the entire geopolitical balance had decisively changed. The only countries left committed to carbon dioxide reductions were now those belonging to the European Union, along with Canada and Australia, between them responsible for just 11.3 percent of total world emissions. The only other Annex 1 countries in the G20 were Japan and Russia, responsible for another 8 percent of global carbon dioxide emissions. And they, like all the other countries that agreed the communiqué after the Hamburg meeting of the G20 in July 2017, had committed themselves to building more coal-fired power stations and thus increasing their emissions.

With that wholly dishonest document, the make-believe of political groupthink over global warming was more damningly exposed than ever before.[103]

But the ultimate irony of all this was that, what had happened in Paris – whether the climate establishment had got its treaty or not – would have had no influence on the future of the earth's climate. This would continue to change, just as it always had done, thanks to that complex interaction of natural factors, such as the shifting cycles in ocean currents and the activity of the sun, the very factors which the scientists carried away by groupthink had long ignored and had never even tried honestly to understand.

The crucial lesson of Paris was that it marked the moment when the groupthink finally and irrevocably began to lose its power. It may continue to hold the Western world in its grip for years to come. But it will become increasingly obvious that the rest of the world, led by the dynamic and fast-growing economies of the East, is taking little notice. In fact, this is only one more reflection of the remarkable geopolitical shift which has lately been taking place. By one measure after another, politically, economically and culturally, we have seen the Western world beginning to lose that pre-eminent place in the world it has enjoyed for several centuries, and the authority that went with it. Other countries, notably China and India, have been moving up to replace and surpass them. China's economy has in recent decades risen to become the second largest in the world, India's is catching up fast, and by one measure is already in fourth place. There are forecasts that by the middle of the century these two most populous countries will not only have the two largest economies, but that India might even overtake China.

There have thus been many signs in recent years that the political power and influence of the West, most notably that of Europe, have been in relative decline. And in this respect the rejection of the West's attempt to get a binding climate treaty in Paris, followed by Trump's withdrawal even from the little that Paris was claimed to have achieved, may well be looked back not just as the moment when the great climate scare finally began to lose it its power. It may be seen as one of the more significant landmarks in a much wider historical process, the nature of which we are only now dimly beginning to recognise, and the full implications of which we cannot yet begin to foresee. Unquestionably we are now entering an entirely new chapter in the story, and one which leaves Europe and Britain looking very uncomfortably isolated. Sooner or later, these new realities crowding in from outside will make it very difficult to sustain the bubble of scientific and political make-believe in which we have been living for so long.

Indeed, this is why it has become more than ever relevant to recognise the real nature of what has been driving this flight from reality for 30 years. It has been a supreme example of the astonishing power of groupthink to carry people off into states of illusion, which, by definition, must always eventually end in disillusionment.

But the belief in man-made climate change is only one of the countless other instances of the power of groupthink in our world today, all similarly behaving according to those rules identified by Irving Janis. That is why I want to end with a personal epilogue briefly referring to other examples of how his analysis can give us a clearer understanding of so much more of what we find puzzling about the strange time we now live in.

23 A personal epilogue: the wider picture

> Men, it has been well said, think in herds; it will be seen that they go mad in herds, while they only recover their senses slowly, and one by one.
>
> Charles Mackay, *Extraordinary Popular Delusions and the Madness of Crowds*

There were two reasons why I was pleased to be asked by the Global Warming Policy Foundation to write this paper. One, as I hope these pages have demonstrated, was that Janis's analysis of groupthink can help us to see in a new light the real nature one of the strangest episodes in human history. But the other was that this has provided an opportunity to show that his thesis has very much greater relevance to our understanding of collective human psychology than has been generally recognised.

One obvious reason is that, to illustrate his theory, he drew only on those few episodes in mid-20th century American political history that were the focus of his study. He showed in each case how a small group of men at the centre of power had become so obsessively fixed on a particular policy that they refused to listen to any evidence that might have raised doubts about what they were agreed on. In each case their failure to consider all its possible consequences led to disaster.

Certainly, more recent history has provided numerous other examples that Janis could have added to his case-studies. One of the more obvious was the recklessly obsessive fashion in which George W. Bush and Tony Blair launched their invasion of Iraq in 2003. So focussed were they on overthrowing Saddam Hussein that they gave no proper thought to what might happen once their goal had been achieved, with the result that Iraq was plunged into years of bloody sectarian chaos.

But what particularly struck me when I first came across Janis's thesis was how much more widely relevant it is to our understanding of collective human behaviour than he was able to demonstrate from just his particular rather limited set of examples (or even than perhaps he himself realised). It can certainly help us to see in a new light the story of global warming, but once we recognise Janis's basic rules of how groupthink operates, we can see other more general instances of it all over the place, both in history and very much in the increasingly puzzling world around us today. We can see how, although most cases of groupthink originate only from a small number of people, those same rules continue to apply when their belief comes to be shared by ever larger numbers of others, who for whatever reason find their belief appealing and are drawn into sharing it by the power of prestige and the contagious power of second-hand thinking.

Precisely because those inside the groupthink bubble cannot think outside it, and look only for evidence which reinforces their belief, it is impossible for them to have any serious dialogue with those who question it. Safe in their bubble, they can thus enjoy a sense of moral superiority over those unenlightened outsiders who disagree with them, who can simply be caricatured as just crazy people, dismissed as not worth listening to.

Any general picture of the part played by groupthink in human affairs must inevitably take account of the fact that, throughout history, few examples have been more extreme than the more fanatical perversions of religion, which is why there is no more obvious example of this today than those terrorist movements inspired by Islamic fundamentalism, such as Isis and Al Qaeda, whose members are transformed by their groupthink into collective psychopaths.

Equally, such a general picture must allow for how the divided world of politics inevitably becomes prey to all kinds of groupthink, large and small; and how this becomes more pronounced the further any group moves towards the 'hard left' or 'hard right' extremes of the political spectrum.

This is never more conspicuous than in those countries where a totalitarian regime seeks to impose its own form of groupthink on an entire population. History provides us with no more dramatic examples than the great revolutionary upheavals that led to such regimes seizing power in the first place, as in England after 1640, France after 1789 and Russia in 1917. Each was originally inspired by a desire to curb the powers of a seemingly oppressive ruling order, but ended up with a new ruling order far worse than the one it replaced.

Even in democracies we can see much less extreme versions of groupthink at work in all sorts of ways. And how often in politics we see two opposing forms of groupthink pitched against each other, as in the unusually fractious US presidential election that led to the election of President Trump or the spectacle of the two rival campaigns in Britain's Brexit referendum, where both sides vied with each other to make equally wild claims that bore little or no relation to reality.

In fact, different forms of groupthink have become such a ubiquitous presence in our time that when I first came across Janis's book I realised that I had unwittingly been writing about examples of it through much of my professional life. One of the strangest and most conspicuous examples has been the rise in recent decades of that intense social pressure to conform with all the multifarious ideological positions which are deemed to be 'politically correct'. This has become the 'New Puritanism' of our time, displaying all the self-righteous certainty we associate with the intolerance of those original Puritans in the 17th century. The sense of moral outrage we associate with political correctness is almost invariably directed at those who can be portrayed as having, through oppression, prejudice or discrimination, turned some other group into a 'victim' – of 'sexism', 'racism', 'homophobia' or whatever.

The same fundamental narrative inspires the views of our more fanatical 'animal rights' campaigners. It also lies behind the way the belief in manmade climate change has become added to the litany of politically correct causes, by seeing the planet itself as a 'victim' which must saved from the evils of 'Big Oil', 'Big Carbon' and all those other malign forces that are threatening it with catastrophic global warming.

My first book back in 1969, was *The Neophiliacs: a study of the revolution in English life in the Fifties and Sixties*. This was an analysis of the explosion of social, moral and cultural change which, in the ten years after 1956, transformed Britain into an almost unrecognisably different country. Only now do I see how much of what I was writing about was shaped by those same rules of groupthink. From the rise of 'pop culture' and the 'permissive society' to Harold Wilson's 'New Britain', much of it was essentially based on different forms of collective make-believe, the consequences of which would turn out to be so different from what had been imagined when that headlong rush into change began.

In 1979 I made a two-hour documentary for the BBC, *City of Towers*, tracing how directly the mess made of Britain's cities in the 1960s by architects, planners and politicians stemmed from the 'brutalist' urban visions of the architect Le Corbusier back in the 1920s. Again, this was a perfect case-study in how groupthink based on make-believe can lead to disastrously unforeseen consequences.

I later wrote books about other subjects on which Janis's thesis can shed revealing new light, ranging from those food scares, such as BSE, which became such a damaging feature of British life in the late-1980s and 1990s (not one of which turned out to be based on proper scientific evidence), to the collective psychology behind that most ambitious political project of our age, the European Union.

And no general account of the power of groupthink these days would be complete without a picture of how it has in recent decades transformed the culture of the BBC. Its relentless propagandising over global warming has been only one of the more glaring symptoms of how the corporation's coverage has become dictated and distorted by a similarly one-sided 'party line' on almost any controversial issue of the day.

But these widely different examples of how people can get caught up groupthink have three things in common. One is that their beliefs always eventually turn out to have been based on a false picture of the world, in some way shaped by the make-believe that it is different from what it really is. The second is the irrational degree of intolerance they display towards those who do not share their beliefs. The third is how ultimately their groupthink must always end up in some way colliding uncomfortably with the reality their blinkered vision has overlooked.

Every South Sea Bubble ends in a crash. Every form of groupthink eventually has its day. This is invariably what happens when human beings get carried along by the crowd, simply because they have lost the urge or ability to think for themselves.

Notes

1. Irving L. Janis, *Victims of Groupthink: A Psychological Study of Foreign Policy Decisions and Fiascoes*, first published in 1972 by Houghton Mifflin Company of Boston, revised and enlarged edition published in 1982 as just *Groupthink*.

2. This was how Bolin was presented, as very much the odd man out, in a two-hour television documentary entitled *The Weather Machine,* shown by the BBC in 1974, in which all the other contributors were predicting the approach of a new ice age.

3. Two earlier scientists predicting that increased human emissions of carbon dioxide could lead to a rise in world temperatures were the Swedish physicist Svante Arrhenius in 1896 and the British meteorologist Guy Callender in 1938 (after noting the rise in temperatures since 1910). Both men suggested that the effects of an increase in atmospheric carbon dioxide could be beneficial, since this would assist plant growth, including food crops. When temperatures declined after 1940, Callender's thesis was largely forgotten, until temperatures again began to rise in the 1970s.

4. Report of the First Session of the WMO/UNEP Intergovernmental Panel on Climate Change, Geneva, 9–11 November 1988. https://www.ipcc.ch/meetings/session01/first-final-report.pdf.

5. It was agreed from the outset that the IPCC's assessment reports would be divided into three parts. Working Group I would be responsible for assessing the science and extent of global warming. Working Group II would focus on its 'impact', Working Group III would consider ways in which that impact could be 'mitigated'. The contributions of Working Groups II and III would be expected to depend on the findings of Working Group I.

6. Two of these were based on surface temperature records. One, jointly produced by John Houghton's new Met Office Hadley Centre and the UEA's Climatic Research Unit was HadCRUt (combining the name of the UK Met Office's Hadley Centre with that of the CRU, plus 't' for temperature); the other was Gistemp, run by James Hansen as director of NASA's Goddard Institute for Space Studies (GISS). Both were therefore run by committed supporters of the 'consensus'. The other two records were based on a completely different system, measurements taken by satellites and balloons. One of these was run by Dr Roy Spencer and Dr John Christy at the University of Alabama in Huntsville, the other, Remote Sensing Systems (RSS) based in California, was a private company contracted to NASA.

7. Richard Lindzen, 'Global warming: the origin and nature of the alleged scientific consensus', *Proceedings of the OPEC Seminar on the Environment, Vienna, 13–15 April 1992* (available on Cato Institute website); also interview with Lindzen, *Die Weltwoche*, 3 March 2007. This section relies heavily on Lindzen's paper, because he was the first major scientist to identify the need, among some, to insist that belief in carbon dioxide-induced global warming was supported by a 'consensus' of scientific opinion, just as he was to remain one of the shrewdest critics of that belief for years to come.

8. Lindzen, *op.cit.*

9. Lindzen, *op.cit.*

10. Houghton J.T. *et al.*(1990), *op.cit.*

11. Friends of the Earth was originally founded in the US in 1969 to protest against nuclear power stations. When Greenpeace was launched by a group of US anti-war protestors in 1971,

their first act had been to try to halt US nuclear weapons testing on an island off Alaska. Its most famous action had been a bid to halt French nuclear weapons tests in the Pacific in 1985, which ended in the sinking of its ship *The Rainbow Warrior* in Auckland Harbour by France's secret service.

12. Lindzen, *op.cit.* Lindzen's view of the petition was that it showed how global warming had become 'part of the dogma of the liberal conscience – a dogma to which scientists are not immune'.

13. Reported in speech to Heartland conference in New York in 2009 by John H. Sununu, who had been chief of staff at the White House to President George H.W. Bush, 1989–1993.

14. At the same time Lindzen was surprised, when invited to a seminar on global warming at another university, to find he was the only scientist on a panel of environmentalists: 'There were strident calls for immediate action and ample expressions of impatience with science'. A congresswoman from Rhode Island acknowledged that 'scientists may disagree, but we can hear Mother Earth, and she is crying'. Lindzen, *op.cit.*

15. Lindzen, *op.cit.*, p. 7.

16. Gore, *op.cit*, p. 40.

17. Letter to Congressman Jim Bates, 14 July 1988. See website of Heartland Institute, article by Fred Singer under 'Environment and Climate News', 1 January 2000.

18. Letter to Senator Tim Wirth, 18 July 1988. Heartland Institute, *op.cit.* See also Fred Singer. 'The Revelle–Gore story: attempted political suppression of science', 2003 (see Hoover website). This account is based largely on Singer's own version, although inevitably this has been attacked by global warming campaigners.

19. *New Republic*, 6 July 1992.

20. These details emerged from a computer disk containing a draft letter sent by Lancaster to Gore (Singer, Hoover, *op.cit.*).

21. Singer himself would be vilified in this way for having participated with Professor Frederick Seitz, a distinguished physicist and former President of the NAS, in a report criticising the efforts of the US Environmental Protection Agency (EPA) to demonise passive smoking. The report's authors were described as 'corrupt' for having 'received funding through 'ideological partners' of tobacco companies'.

22. Twelve years later, in 2004, Lancaster issued a 'retraction' of his 'retraction' on a website ('The *Cosmos Myth*'). However, he omitted any reference to the evidence which had come to light during the discovery process of the legal action. This included his admission that Revelle had told him that he agreed with the main point the article sought to make: that the science on global warming was not yet sufficiently settled to justify drastic action.

23. The authors of this report, published by Pantheon Books, New York, 1991, were Alexander King and Bertrand Schneider, the president and general secretary of the Club of Rome, updating the message of its best-selling book in the 1970s, *The Limits to Growth*.

24. *Wall Street Journal*, 12 June 1996

25. John Houghton, 'Meetings that changed the world', *Nature*, 9 October 2008

26. *Wall Street Journal*, 12 June 1996.

27. Paul N. Edwards and Stephen H.Schneider, 'The 1995 IPCC report: broad consensus or 'scientific cleansing'?', *Ecofable/Ecoscience* 1.1.(1997), pp. 3–9

28. Schneider also insisted that 'nowhere do IPCC rules explicitly address the question of when a report chapter becomes final (i.e. when all changes must cease)' and that Santer's conduct had been entirely within the 'spirit' of the IPCC process, (Schneider *op.cit*, p. 6).
29. Singer and Avery, *op.cit.* This political background to the IPCC's 1996 report emerged in evidence given to the US House Committee on Small Business, chaired by Congressman James Talent, in August 1998.
30. A graph showing the Middle Ages as significantly warmer than the late 20th century had been published in the first IPCC report in 1990, attributed to John Houghton himself, although he had adapted it from one created by the distinguished climate historian Professor Hubert Lamb, the first director of the University of East Anglia's CRU. It was he who first identified the Medieval Warm Period (although he originally called it the Medieval Warm Epoch).
31. The two fullest accounts of how the methods used to concoct the 'hockey stick' graph came to be exposed were by Andrew Montford, *The Hockey Stick Illusion* (2010) and also *Hiding the Decline* (2012). For a summary, see Christopher Booker, *The Real Global Warming Disaster* (2009).
32. For once, Dr Richard Lindzen was able to testify on the 2001 report as an insider, because he had worked on it as a lead author. He explained to a Senate committee how, as in 1995, the Summary had again been significantly modified after the contributing scientists had signed it off, to remove any suggestions of uncertainty or disagreement. He also described the pressure contributors had been put under by 'IPCC co-ordinators', who would 'go round insisting that criticism of models be toned down'; and that 'refusals were occasionally met with *ad hominem* attacks. I personally witnessed co-authors forced to assert their 'green' credentials in defence of their statements'. (Testimony to Senate Commerce Committee, 1 May 2001).
33. In Mann's original paper, the use of two different datasets was discernable, if somewhat unclear.
34. In fact two earlier attempts had been made to show that the 'hockey stick' was scientifically quite implausible, using very different methods. Dr Willie Soon and Dr Sallie Baliunas of the Harvard-Smithsonian Institute of Astrophysics had in 2003 published the findings of an exhaustive meta-analysis of 140 academic papers that used 'proxies' to reconstruct past temperatures. 116 confirmed the existence of the Medieval Warm Period, and only seven failed to show it. John Daly had published on his Australian website a mass of historical evidence to show that the Medieval Warm Period did exist. As the Climategate emails were to reveal, these researches also made Soon, Baliunas and Daly into 'hate-figures' for Mann and his co-authors of the emails.
35. For a full account of the story see Andrew Montford's *The Hockey Stick Illusion*, Stacey International, 2010.
36. In fact Pachauri had already been involved in a curious episode in 2004, when Kevin Trenberth, one of the little group of scientists at the top of the IPCC and a Working Group I Lead Author, had invited Dr Chris Landsea, the unrivalled expert on Atlantic hurricanes, to contribute to the next IPCC report. Soon after accepting, Landsea had been astonished to learn from a press release that Trenberth was to give a wildly alarmist presentation claiming that hurricane activity was increasing. Landsea wrote to him to explain that not a single study had supported such a view. Trenberth carried on regardless, winning widespread publicity for his claim. When Landsea protested to various senior IPCC figures, its chairman Pachauri replied that Trenberth

had every right to express his views on hurricanes, and that these were similar to what the IPCC had said in its 2001 report (to which Landsea had contributed). Landsea replied that he could no longer contribute to 'a process that I view as being motivated by a preconceived agenda and being scientifically unsound'. He resigned.

37. The most obvious historical exception was what had happened in every country taken over by a communist government, where of course its entire society was compelled to follow 'correct thinking' on all issues, including science.

38. Evidence given by King to the Commons Environmental Audit Committee, 30 March 2004. See also 'Antarctica will soon be the only place to live', interview with King, *The Independent*, 2 May 2004.

39. See transcript of press conference given by Alexander Illarionov on 8 July 2004, available on http://www.rightsidenews.com/200807241524/energy-and-environment/results-of-the-climate-change-and-kyoto-protocol-seminar-in-moscow.html and other internet sources. Also 'Bad manners at the Moscow Kyoto Protocol seminar', *Financial Post*, 13 July 2004.

40. Richard D. North is not to be confused with Dr Richard A.E. North who features later in this paper.

41. Written evidence by Rosemary Righter to House of Lords Select Committee on Economic Affairs, Vol. II, July 2005.

42. 'Now the Pentagon tells Bush: Climate change will destroy us', *Observer*, 11 November 2004.

43. Analysis originally published on his website by Dr Benny Peiser, when he was working at John Moores University. He subsequently became director of the Global Warming Policy Foundation, publishers of this paper.

44. '*Gristmill, the environmental news blog*', 19 September 2006.

45. Later in the year, because of this, a High Court action was brought against the government under two sections of the Education Act, which ordained that controversial or political material could only be used in schools so long as 'balancing material was used to show the other side of the argument'. The judge ruled that the film could continue to be shown to students, but that nine points in it had been demonstrated to be so incorrect that this was only to be allowed on condition that the schools were supplied with material explaining this. The Department of Education complied by sending out a statement 77 pages long. Not one teacher I spoke to from schools where the DVD was shown had ever seen this document.

46. The other satellite record was kept by Remote Sensing Systems (RSS), a private company contracted to NASA.

47. Svensmark had been working with Friis-Christensen, director of the Danish National Space Centre, on a mechanism whereby fluctuations in solar activity, by changing the amount of cosmic rays hitting the Earth, could influence the formation of cloud cover. More clouds led to a cooler earth and vice versa. The results of his experiments were striking (but were dismissed by Bert Bolin as 'scientifically extremely naïve and irresponsible'). Four months after Svensmark's work was featured on *The Great Global Warming Swindle*, the Royal Society, *Nature* and the BBC joined forces to publicise a paper claiming to have demolished his theory. Some years later, experiments at CERN confirmed that it was correct.

48. The story behind *The Great Global Warming Swindle* had begun the previous year when its producer Martin Durkin was present at a meeting in Tokyo of the World Congress of Science Pro-

ducers. He asked why the world's major television networks were paying so little attention to the serious doubts being raised by reputable scientists about the 'consensus' on global warming. This prompted an angry response from a senior BBC science producer, Michael Mosley, insisting that not a single serious scientist disagreed with the 'consensus'. So fierce were the ensuing exchanges that it was agreed that Durkin and Mosley should debate the issue at the Congress's next meeting in New York. Here Durkin argued his case so effectively that many other producers present agreed he had a point. Their reaction persuaded Channel 4 to commission Durkin to make the film, broadcast on 8 March 2007.

49. Hansen, J.E. and S. Lebedeff, 1987: Global trends of measured surface air temperature. *J. Geophys. Res.*, 92, 13345–13372

50. One former world leader who had already rejected the IPCC's position was Mrs Thatcher, long acclaimed by supporters of the 'consensus' as the first to have given it influential support in 1988. In her last book, *Statecraft,* in 2003, she devoted several pages to a total recantation of her earlier view. She voiced precisely the fundamental doubts about the 'consensus' which were later to become so familiar. Pouring scorn on the 'doomsters', she now questioned the assumption that the chief factor shaping world climate was carbon dioxide, rather than natural factors, such as solar activity. She mocked Al Gore and the futility of the costly and economically damaging schemes being advanced to reduce carbon dioxide emissions. She cited the Medieval Warm Period as having had entirely beneficial effects. And she recognised how distortions of the science had been used to mask an anti-capitalist, left-wing political agenda that posed a serious threat to the progress and prosperity of mankind. Not one newspaper reported this remarkable U-turn by the lady 'not for turning', and seven years later David Cameron was still being praised by supporters of the 'consensus' as a true 'Thatcherite' for his 'green' policies on climate change. See 'Hot air and global warming', Lady Thatcher, *Statecraft* pp. 449–456 and Christopher Booker, 'Was Mrs Thatcher the first 'climate sceptic'?', *Sunday Telegraph*, 10 June 2010:

51. For a YouTube interview in which Worthington tells the story behind the Climate Change Act, see https://www.youtube.com/watch?v=X3xseCcfMZY.

52. For example, Jones's response to a request from Warwick Hughes in 2004: 'Why should I make this data available to you when your aim is to try and find something wrong with it' (email 1299).

53. 'The UK Information Commissioner said that 'more cogent prima facie evidence of an offence under the FOI Act was impossible to contemplate', but noted that a statute of limitations limited their jurisdiction'. 'New light on "delete any emails"', *Climate Audit*, 23 February 2011.

54. Dr R.K. Pachauri quoted in the *Times of India*, 1 November 2009, http://timesofindia.indiatimes.com/india/No-proof-of-Himalayan-ice-melting-due-to-climate-change/articleshow/5213045.cms.

55. John McLean, 'Prejudiced authors, prejudiced findings', Science and Public Policy Institute, 2008.

56. No one did more to unearth the true origins of these claims than Dr Richard A.E. North (not to be confused with Richard D. North mentioned earlier). Dr North's expert researches were the basis for the exposure of 'Glaciergate' in the *Sunday Times* and my own column in the *Sunday Telegraph,* and for my subsequent columns on the IPCC's claims over the Amazon and African

crop yields (see below): as they were also for our joint-articles in the *Sunday Telegraph* on the financial affairs of Dr Pachauri.

57. Laframboise later published a full account of this study in a book, *The Delinquent Teenager who was Mistaken for the World's Top Climate Expert*, Kindle edition, 2011.

58. TERI commissioned KPMG to carry out an 'informal audit' of Pachauri's finances, which reported that 'no evidence was found that indicated personal financial benefits accruing to Dr Pachauri from his various advisory roles that would have led to a conflict of interest'.

59. 'Phil Jones: Q and A'. BBC News website, 13 February 2010.

60. The only exceptions were Lord Lawson and Dr Benny Peiser representing the Global Warming Policy Foundation, the London-based think-tank set up in 2009 as part of the science-based 'counter-consensus' which had been emerging in Britain and the USA.

61. The five inquiries in the US all came to similar conclusions.

62. In 2015 Pachauri faced allegations of sexual harassment and criminal intimidation by a young female employee of TERI. He was later given bail by the Delhi High Court while these charges were formally investigated by the police. He resigned from TERI later that year.

63. See 'Sir John Beddington warns of floods, droughts and storms', *BBC News* website, 25 March 2013. Like his predecessors as chief scientific adviser, Lord May and Sir David King, Beddington had no qualifications in climate science; his specialities were the computer modelling of 'population biology' and the 'sustainable use of renewable resources'.

64. The flooding of Brisbane in January 2011 had only become a disaster through the sudden release of a huge volume of water from an upstream reservoir, which local politicians had insisted must be kept full, because they had been advised that global warming would bring prolonged droughts. The rains forced them to open the floodgates.

65. In September 2017 there was to be a replay of these attempts to link extreme weather events with climate change, following the arrival in the Western Hemisphere of hurricanes Harvey and Irma, the first major hurricanes to make US landfall for 11 years. Both storms were claimed to be 'unprecedented', and media headlines claimed that Irma was 'the most powerful hurricane on record' and 'the deadliest storm in history'. Neither claim was remotely true. Irma's maximum windspeed of 185mph had been equalled twice in the past 37 years alone and beaten in 1980. It ended up causing 36 deaths, whereas even since 1980 there have been hurricanes which killed 1100 and 8000 people in Central America. But this hysteria prompted the BBC and others repeatedly to claim that such hurricanes were becoming 'more frequent' and were evidence of man-made climate change. The BBC *Today* programme even staged a discussion between a former director of Friends of the Earth and the head of an Oxford University 'Climate Dynamics Group' on whether the world's top 19 carbon dioxide-emitting companies could be made to pay for clearing up all the damage Irma had caused.

66. The *Independent* was the paper which in 2000 had famously quoted Dr David Viner, a senior scientist at the CRU, as saying that within a few years snow in Britain would be 'a very rare and exciting event' and that 'children just aren't going to know what snow is'.

67. See, for instance, post on the NASA website dated 30 October 2013 reporting its satellite data having shown that between 1992 and 2001 the Antarctic ice sheet registered 'a net gain of 112 billion tons of ice a year', which had slowed between 2003 and 2012 to '82 billion tons of

ice per year'. https://www.nasa.gov/feature/goddard/nasa-study-mass-gains-of-antarctic-ice-sheet-greater-than-losses.

68. Slingo's actual wording was 'the model that we use for our climate prediction work and our weather forecasts, the unified model'. http://www.publications.parliament.uk/pa/cm200910/cmselect/cmsctech/387/387ii.pdf.

69. *Uncertainty, Risk and Dangerous Climate Change* published by the Hadley Centre in December 2004: http://www.metoffice.gov.uk/media/pdf/l/1/COP10.pdf.

70. On 9 February 2014 the BBC website quoted Slingo as saying that the UK was experiencing the 'most exceptional period of rainfall in 248 years...we have records going back to 1766 and we have nothing like this,' http://www.bbc.co.uk/news/uk-politics-26084625. Yet the Met Office's own historical UK rainfall data showed that the 544.8 mm which fell in the three months up to February 2014 was still less than the 554 mm recorded between November 1929 and January 1930.

71. The only MP to question the Met Office's record was, again, Peter Lilley. On an otherwise fairly light-hearted BBC programme presented in August 2015 by the *Daily Mail*'s humorous parliamentary sketchwriter Quentin Letts, entitled 'What's the point of the Met Office?', Lilley mocked the failure of the temperature predictions made in its 2004 report. This prompted a fine example of psychological projection from the BBC's former science editor Richard Black, whose partisan reporting on climate change had long been a byword. He complained in the *Guardian* that the programme had breached the BBC's commitment to impartiality. Two months later the BBC apologised for the 'unfortunate lapse' by which the programme had 'failed to meet our editorial standards'. See 'The BBC apologises for documentary that criticised the Met Office over climate change', The *Independent*, 7 October 2015.

72. For fuller analysis, see '97 percent cooked stats' by Lawrence Solomon, *Financial Post*, 3 January 2011.

73. 'Debunking climate propaganda earns you a fail', Christopher Booker, *Sunday Telegraph*, 6 October 2012. For a wider look at how the 'consensus' orthodoxy had permeated Britain's education system, see also Andrew Montford and John Shade, *Climate Control: Brainwashing in Schools* (Global Warming Policy Foundation, April 2014).

74. Although each of these were analysed at the end of my report for the GWPF in 2011 (*op. cit.*), it is appropriate to summarise them more briefly here because they so tellingly revealed just how completely the BBC had fallen into the grip of evangelistic groupthink.

75. Later in the programme, Delingpole was given similar treatment. From three hours of filming at his home, two clips were picked out. In one, Nurse was shown suggesting to him that, if a 'consensus' of doctors agreed he had cancer, he would not question it. Why therefore should he question the scientific consensus on global warming? When Delingpole momentarily looked nonplussed by the absurdity of this analogy, the programme had got what it wanted. In the other clip, Delingpole explained that he did not 'read peer-reviewed papers' on climate change, because he read commentaries on them by experts better qualified than himself to understand them. Delingpole could thus be shown admitting that he did not read or understand 'peer-reviewed science'. Again the programme had got what it wanted.

76. Editorial control over all matters relating to climate change at Wikipedia had long been taken over by fervent advocates for the 'consensus', who ruthlessly ensured that the contents of

the world's most influential information source rigorously conformed with the 'party line'. This included highly critical entries on all prominent 'deniers'. A key role was played by William Connolley, a British climate activist (and a co-founder with Michael Mann of the *RealClimate* website), who enjoyed the status of a 'senior editor' and 'administrator'. In 2009 Lawrence Solomon, a Canadian journalist with the *National Post,* revealed that Connolley had created or re-written '5428 unique Wikipedia articles' on climate change, deleted 'over 500' and barred more than 2000 contributors from its pages. This revelation of the power he exercised created such a scandal that in 2010 Connolley was barred from making any further contributions on subjects related to climate change or exercising any control over Wikipedia's contents.

77. The day after Jones's report was published, the *Daily Mail* serialised the memoirs of a much-respected former BBC newsreader, Peter Sissons, under the headline 'The BBC became a propaganda machine for climate change...and I was treated like a lunatic for daring to dissent' (*Daily Mail*, 9 February 2011).

78. The surface data were in fact initially supplied to the GHCN, part of the National Climate Data Center, which was in turn part of NOAA, under the US Government's Department of Commerce. With the addition of further data. These were further processed and published by GISS, and also contributed to the HadCRUT temperature record.

79. See 'Historical station distribution' on *Climate Audit*, 2 October 2008; and *'Surface Temperature Records: A Policy-Driven Deception?'* by Joseph d'Aleo and Anthony Watts, Science and Public Policy Institute, 2010.

80. For analysis and charts, see 'RSS continues to diverge from GISS' and 'Records and Adjustments' (4 and 6 December 2014) on Paul Homewood's blog, *Notalotofpeopleknowthat*. See also his posts under 'Temperature adjustments'.

81. In 2017 Homewood was attacked in a book on 'climate denial' published in the US (repeated in a laudatory review in the *Washington Post*) for having 'offered no evidence to back up his incendiary claim of massive temperature tampering'. In fact, every one of his posts was illustrated with 'before and after' graphs, comparing the original with the adjusted data, all meticulously based on and linked to GISS's own archive. This can be seen on his website, *Notalotofpeopleknowthat*, by clicking on 'Temperature adjustment' in the subject list on the right, then scrolling down to 'Massive tampering with data in South America' (20 January 2015), and many subsequent posts.

82. For a detailed account of this story, see 'New Zealand NIWA temperature train wreck' posted in October 2010 on *Watts Up With That?* This blog had long played a significant role in exposing the systematic fiddling of temperature data, as had the US mathematician Tony Heller on his blog *Real Science* and Dr Jennifer Marohasy in Australia,

83. When McIntyre questioned Gavin Schmidt at GISS about this, the earlier version was quickly reinstated. Eight years later, the much greater range of 'adjustments' affecting GISS, NOAA, the GHCN and HadCRUt, all remained in place.

84. Interestingly, in 2017 two Australian scientists reported that almost exactly the same trick had been played with the main record of sea levels, the Permanent Service for Mean Sea Levels (PSMSL). Using three data records for the Indian Ocean, Dr Albert Parker and Dr Clifford Ollier showed how, in each case, significant 'corrections' had been made, to give the 'spurious' impression that sea levels originally recorded as stable or falling had instead been sharply rising. This

had been done by the familiar technique of lowering the data for earlier years and increasing that for recent years. Observing that 'It is always highly questionable to shift data collected in the far past without any proven new supporting material', the authors concluded that 'the data-adjusters at PSMSL are attempting to "correct" the sea level rise data that do not support the conceptualization of a rapidly-rising sea level trend in response to rising human CO_2 emissions'. See Parker and Ollier, 'Are the sea levels stable at Aden, Yemen?'. *Earth Systems and Environment*, 2017; 1: 18.

85. 'Paris deal a "turning point" in global warming fight, Obama says', *Guardian*, 5 October 2016.

86. The story of how Pope Francis was persuaded to lend the global 'prestige' of his office to this document was not irrelevant to our theme. The passages in the encyclical *Laudate Si* dealing with global warming were based almost entirely on a briefing from a body called the Pontifical Academy of Sciences. Its chief adviser on climate was one of the most vocal advocates of climate alarmism, Professor Hans Schellnhuber, director of the Potsdam Institute for Climate Impact. This was why the Pope's letter referred to several of the familiar memes in the standard warmist litany: tipping points, ocean acidification, melting polar ice caps and so on. But Schellnhuber, it was reported, had been recruited for the task by the Argentine bishop appointed by Pope Francis to be Chancellor of the Pontifical Academy of Sciences, Marcello Sanchez Sorrondo, who was reported as dismissing any scientists dissenting from the climate orthodoxy as being 'funded by the oil industry'.

87. The man initially responsible for this analysis was again Paul Homewood. For his detailed reports on each of these INDCs, with sources, see his blog *Notalotofpeopleknowthat*. Click on 'Paris' in the index on the right, then scroll down to 'older posts' between 2 October and 30 November 2015.

88. Thanks to Paul Homewood's researches, chronicled on his blog, it was possible to report all this more than a month before the Paris conference began, as I did in the *Sunday Telegraph* on 31 October 2015 http://www.telegraph.co.uk/comment/11968064/Why-the-Paris-climate-treaty-will-be-the-flop-of-the-year.html. No other newspaper reported any of these facts, although all were freely available on the internet.

89. See Booker, 'The Paris climate fiasco leaves UK alone in the dark', *Sunday Telegraph*, 19 December 2015.

90. Key World Energy Statistics 2016, International Energy Agency.

91. Despite this, it had now become customary for supporters of the 'consensus' to claim that renewable energy was now becoming so much cheaper, and that fossil fuels were being so heavily subsidised that renewable energy would soon be competitive with them. To justify these claims called for such prestidigitation with the figures that few apart from paid propagandists for the 'consensus' were taken in by them.

92. There is a common confusion (see reference to Tony Blair earlier) between energy and electricity. Electricity represents less than a fifth of all energy consumed, which also includes gas for heating and cooking, coal for industry and heating, and oil for most forms of transport. The vast majority of energy thus comes from fossil fuels.

93. Although in 2011 the European Commission had published its *Energy Roadmap* setting a similar 80 percent reduction target by 2050, with reductions of 20 percent by 2020, 40 percent by 2030 and 60 percent by 2040, this did not have the force of law.

94. See report by Office for Budget Responsibility on http://budgetresponsibility.org.uk/efo/economic-fiscal-outlook-march-2017/. Apart from the way windfarms had come to dominate significant parts of Britain's landscape, several studies in Britain and abroad had shown the damage the windmills did to birds and bats, including species, such as golden eagles, which the law was meant to protect.
95. Although Marxism of course had laid claim to this with its doctrine of 'scientific materialism'.
96. See for instance N. Keenlyside *et al.* (2008) 'Advancing decadal-scale climate predictions in the North Atlantic sector', *Nature*, 453, 84–88. This paper accepted that the IPCC's forecast of a 0.3°C temperature rise during the current decade had not been confirmed by the evidence. But this, Keenlyside conceded, was because its models were not programmed to take account of ocean currents such as the Gulf Stream. He nevertheless insisted that his own model confirmed that by 2015 the warming caused by carbon dioxide would re-assert itself, carrying temperatures up to record levels.
97. The IPCC based its claim on two papers. The first, by Church *et al.*, (*Geophysical Research Letters*, 16 September 2011), was led by John Church, who had long been the most prominent advocate for the 'consensus' view on sea-levels. This was followed by Levitus *et al.*, (in the same journal, 17 May 2012). The 93% claim came from the latter paper. These papers were greeted with huge relief by the 'consensus' as providing a wholly new explanation for the pause in temperatures. By the time of the El Niño spike in 2016 this was enabling them to claim that the pause had never existed - until temperatures again dropped.
98. See account of 2004 Moscow conference, *op.cit.*
99. How appropriate it was that when Strong had to retire in disgrace to Beijing, after being caught out benefiting from an Iraqi 'food for oil' scandal, he should have been employed in setting up China's first 'carbon exchange' to trade in carbon credits. Equally apt was the timing of his death back in Canada on 27 November 2015, just days before the Paris conference began.
100. See 'An inconvenient truth: "Climate change industry" now a $1.5 trillion global business', *Washington Times*, 11 August 2015.
101. When I sent a draft of this paper to a senior executive in a world-leading engineering firm, he said that even in his organisation 'the catastrophic impact of manmade carbon dioxide on climate has swept all before it and is unchallengeable. Our "green policies" are focused unquestioningly on carbon reduction being the objective, much more than other sustainable practices. If you question the consensus you are clearly (i) not of right mind as the facts are "indisputable", and (ii) a bad person to boot. Obviously you are not wanting to save the planet'.
102. For calculations of the actual figures, see 'Paris won't stop carbon dioxide emissions rising', P. Homewood, *Notalotofpeopleknowthat*, 17 November 2015. The more precise figures he extracted from the INDCs were, for the US and the EU a drop of 1,856 Mt of carbon dioxide, for India an increase of 4,895 Mt, and for China 10,871 Mt.
103. Figures published by Paul Homewood, taken from the Carbon Dioxide Information Analysis Center (CDIAC), run by the US Department of Energy, See 'G20: Leaders fail to bridge Trump climate chasm', *Notalotofpeopleknowthat*, 9 July 2017.

About the Global Warming Policy Foundation

The Global Warming Policy Foundation is an all-party and non-party think tank and a registered educational charity which, while openminded on the contested science of global warming, is deeply concerned about the costs and other implications of many of the policies currently being advocated.

Our main focus is to analyse global warming policies and their economic and other implications. Our aim is to provide the most robust and reliable economic analysis and advice. Above all we seek to inform the media, politicians and the public, in a newsworthy way, on the subject in general and on the misinformation to which they are all too frequently being subjected at the present time.

The key to the success of the GWPF is the trust and credibility that we have earned in the eyes of a growing number of policy makers, journalists and the interested public. The GWPF is funded overwhelmingly by voluntary donations from a number of private individuals and charitable trusts. In order to make clear its complete independence, it does not accept gifts from either energy companies or anyone with a significant interest in an energy company.

Printed in Great Britain
by Amazon

59790138R00061